THAT'S BULLSHIT

About the Author

Mark Bramwell's experience spans the fields of organisation dynamics, employee engagement, leadership capability and interpersonal communications. As an executive coach, trainer and facilitator, Masters qualified in Organisational Psychology, Mark has spent the last 20 years working with a diverse range of organisations and individuals.

Through his work he has observed the negative impact caused by a plethora of bullshit advice, bullshit leadership practices, and bullshit communication habits.

He has witnessed the destructive toll on mental health and wellbeing from an ever-louder message that presents success as being wholly measured by an endless pursuit of more – the growing expectation that success can only be had if we forever get more, have more and be more!

In 2007, Mark created *Bramwell Solutions*. His aim was to break free of the corporate rat race and offer clients a genuine and authentic consulting approach – an approach free of smoke and mirrors, and free of slick sales pitches. To focus on offering advice and expertise that would assist organisations and their staff reach their full potential and achieve a rewarding balance between personal wellbeing, job satisfaction and life success. To tell clients what they needed to hear, not just what they wanted to hear.

www.bramwellsolutions.com.au

That's Bullshit

Stop drowning under stress-inducing advice and a relentless pursuit of more

MARK BRAMWELL

Bramwell Solutions

Copyright © 2020 by Mark Bramwell

All rights reserved. No part of this book may be reproduced in any manner whatsoever without written permission except in the case of brief quotations embodied in critical articles and reviews.

First Printing, 2020

Thank you to my wife Maria for calling out my own bullshit from the first day we met.

Thank you to my beautiful children, Kasper and Anna, for politely laughing at my bullshit dad jokes, but always reminding me when I have gone too far.

And thank you to my parents, Tom and Trish, for planting the bullshit calling seed – for teaching me to never be afraid to disagree and stand up for what I believe in.

Contents

About The Author   ii
Dedication   v

Part 1: The Problem With Bullshit   1

  1   Introduction   3

  2   In the Beginning – My Own (Bullshit) Self-Discovery   11

  3   The Growth of Bullshit   21

Part 2: Identifying And Removing The Bullshit   33

  4   When Enough is No Longer Enough   35

  5   The Alternative - Recalibrate: "Enough is Enough"   43

  6   Self-Obsession is not Self-Awareness   55

  7   The Alternative - The Beginnings of Self-Awareness   65

  8   The Misuse of Assertiveness   79

  9   The Alternative - Modern Assertiveness   91

10	Loving the Sound of Your Own Voice	103
11	The Alternative - Effective Listening and Questioning	113
12	Annoying "Inspirational" Statements	131
13	The Alternative - Defining Statements	141
14	Work-Life Balance	149
15	The Alternative - Finding Your Personal Sweet Spot	157

Part 3: Specific Areas Abundant With Bullshit — 169

16	The Over-Complication of Leadership	171
17	The Alternative - Authentic Leadership	183
18	Lack of Responsiveness	191
19	The Alternative - Developing a Responsive Mindset	197
20	The Misinterpretation of Body Language	205
21	The Alternative - Context and Patterns	213
22	In Conclusion - The Way Forward	221

Part 1: The Problem with Bullshit

The insidious negative impact bullshit advice and excessive expectation setting has had on creating imbalanced and stress-filled lives.

Chapter 1

Introduction

The Challenge

This book represents the culmination of my professional journey, experiences and life learnings.

Over the years I have encountered a myriad of advice: "hot tips" for instant life success, academic studies and everything in-between. But, included in this advice has been an overabundance of bullshit.

Bullshit served up by so-called "experts" that heightens our stress and anxiety levels by creating an exhausting state of mind. The creation of an endless pursuit of *more,* driven by what are too frequently, meaningless, stress-inducing and ridiculous expectation setting messages.

A pursuit that, if we are not careful, will leave us feeling as though we will never have enough, achieve enough or *be* enough.

It is exhausting to always be looking forward. To always be working towards getting what we don't have yet. It is time to stop and better appreciate and also celebrate where we have come from, where we have reached, and what we have already achieved.

For this to be possible, we must be better skilled at critically evaluating many of the messages and pressures that modern life places on us. To explore how to shift our focus away from the modern-day bullshit feed of pursuing *more, more, more,* and focus instead on creating a truly healthier, happier, and sustainable lifestyle.

We should definitely continue to work at being the best possible version of ourselves.

But, it should be a version *we* define. A version that *we* can feel proud of achieving. A version that is self-aware. We should determine what success looks and feels like according to our own definition and goals, rather than assessing the value and quality of our actions by the teachings of self-proclaimed "experts," or always feeling there was something even better to have accomplished instead.

Advice that drives the setting of vague, over-ambitious or unachievable goals is bullshit we must rid from our lives. Anything that causes a deviation from a healthy path of self-discovery and self-development is unwanted.

Finding Balance

We need to strike a better and more sustainable balance in all that we do. Balance in how we live, in how we communicate, in what we take from, and give back to, our environment and our communities.

We need to find a better-balanced self-perception that doesn't make unrealistic comparisons against highly filtered and morphed representations of who we think we *should be*, or worse still, against ridiculous representations others attempt to convince us we *must be*.

The impact of imbalance on our lives can vary substantially. For the more extremely impacted, it may manifest as a constant state of exhaustion, perhaps a degree of self-loathing, or perhaps elements of feeling like a fraud and a failure. For many the imbalance is only slight. Here, the impact may be heightened levels of stress, perhaps anxiety as we approach our limits, or perhaps simply a sense that we have had enough of what modern life sells us.

To achieve a rewarding life, we must stop allowing excessive expectations to induce stress and escalate our fears of falling short. But to achieve this, the flow of bullshit must first be stemmed. We must cease the narrative that drives us to compete and compete – not only against others, but also with ourselves. A narrative where anything short of amazing kick-arse success across all facets of our life is presented as a failure.

We must call 'ENOUGH!'

I'm not suggesting we simply lower or remove our personal goals and aspirations. Far from it. Instead, we must reconsider our approach, and have in place an appropriate, realistic and *meaningful* set of expectations. Expectations that are founded on a holistic and constructive view of our personal needs, capability and priorities. Not expectations shoved down our throats by strangers who claim that they alone know what will make us happy.

To strike a better balance, we also need to stop swinging widely from one self-help approach or methodology to another. This approach is unsustainable. When we see something that is presented as the brilliant new way forward, we can far too frequently throw ourselves into its pursuit before fully evaluating its merit, its personal relevance, or its suitability.

We need to view the achievement of balance in life as similar to the movement of a delicate pendulum. The right amount, the perfect point to be aiming for, is the *exact* midpoint of the pendulum's arc. The sweet spot right in the middle. The balance point. By finding that sweet spot in our behaviours, actions, and ideas we are finding the perfect combination of what really matters. What is excessive? What is insufficient?

Many of the consumer-driven messages that assail our senses focus on our insecurities. They play on our need to keep up with others by having the latest gadgets, the shiniest car, or a bigger house. While the self-help industry leverages these insecurities by jumping in and relentlessly peddling the mantra that 'you can be whatever you want to be.'

And so, in we leap and the pendulum swings widely backwards and forwards as we seek that secret to success. But I call bullshit. How much of this advice is constructive? How much really promotes the pursuit of activities that will genuinely enrich our lives? How much promotes dreams that are within the realms of our personal capability to achieve?

By removing bullshit advice, and a relentless pursuit of more from our lives, we can ensure we define and set our own goals, aspirations and dreams at levels that are personally relevant, meaningful, inspiring *and* achievable.

A Bullshit Assessment

Consider your bullshit detecting ability by taking the *Bullshit-O-Meter* assessment.

Are you a person who is prone to believing bullshit? Alternatively, are you a supreme sceptic who can sniff out bullshit from a mile away? Can you discern slick sales pitches and false promises from genuine facts and insights that will add real benefit and value to your life? Can you distinguish between someone who is trying to use you to achieve their own means, from someone who is genuine in their offer of support? Can you differentiate a leader who only revels in their own success, from one who revels in the success they support others to achieve?

To assess your bullshit-identifying capability, consider the following statements.

Rate yourself for each on a scale of 1 to 5. But be honest – no bullshitting allowed.

SCALE
1. Absolutely
2. Usually
3. Sometimes
4. That might be a bit of a bullshit thing to do
5. That is definitely a bullshit thing to do

STATEMENTS

1. I believe everything I read.

2. I trust that others will always have my best interests in mind.

3. The internet is only full of valuable and insightful content.

4. All inspirational statements make complete sense and are applicable to everyone.

5. The exclusive pursuit of personal goals that are solely focused on getting what you want is exactly what the world needs.

6. All experts who contact me to offer help are only doing so out of the goodness of their hearts.

7. Following the latest fad is the best thing to do. Waiting until something has been proven through improved outcomes

and/or scientific research is only missing the opportunity to get in early and lead the way.

8. Great leaders always keep their office door open to convey their approachability.

9. Once someone has responded to a request, it is a legitimate and professional communication strategy to ignore their further communications and no longer acknowledge their existence.

10. I should *never* cross my arms as it *always* conveys defensiveness.

SCORING
Now add up your responses to get your score. Next, find the range your score falls within below to understand your current bullshit detecting capability.

Score 10 – 20: I'm glad you are reading his book. You need it. Your ability to detect bullshit needs some serious work. You are likely highly gullible. You endlessly pursue fads and swallow meaningless inspirational statements without chewing.

Score 21 – 30: You appear to have some ability to detect the presence of bullshit. But you seriously lack the ability to clearly determine where the smell is emanating from. You are likely to pursue pointless and shallow advice without first evaluating its merit.

Score 31 – 40: You have a reasonable sense of bullshit detection. You do, however, need to hone these skills to better distinguish between fact and fiction. You may be able to detect bullshit, but at times you can be caught out by subtle versions of rubbish advice nicely wrapped up in marketing hype.

Score 41 – 50: Your *Bullshit-O-Meter* is well refined. This book will help to reaffirm concepts and a mindset you already grasp. It will provide you with further ideas for how to influence others to improve their bullshit detection capability. You have the skill to join me and become an anti-bullshit campaigner to help rid the world of this modern-day affliction.

What Does it Mean?

Of course, *The Bullshit-O-Meter* is not a robust and valid assessment of your ability to detect bullshit, but it should have started you thinking about your current mindset toward external advice and your ensuing reactions.

Are you sufficiently critical of your surrounds, the advice you receive, and your communication practices and beliefs?

The lower the score, the more likely you are to wildly swing from one fad to another, while poorly assessing the merit and validity of proffered advice. The higher the score, the more likely you are skilled at adopting an analytical approach. To better discern constructive and beneficial information from the fast-talking sales pitch.

The Way Forward

This book focuses on building your mindset and skills to achieve the latter. It focuses on critically reviewing areas of modern life that are now overflowing with an abundance of bullshit misinformation. Misinformation that drives excessive stress, pressure or poor practice. Alternative approaches are provided to support creating a balanced, accurate and constructive self-perception, and creating habits that will lead to a balanced, positive and rewarding life.

As you read on, step back and reassess your mindset, self-awareness, personal goals, and communication practices. Challenge yourself to critically evaluate the advice and information you have used to create your goals, your aspirations, or your personal leadership and communication style. In doing so, remind yourself of what is most important to *you* – but as defined by *you*, not as defined by unrelenting external expectations to forever get more, go-further and aim higher.

Finding Your Harbour

I have often imagined that running my own business is like a yachtsman constantly searching for the next gust of wind to take me forward. When there is a lull, I become restless and worried and impatiently search the horizon. But the moment a new gust fills my sails, the excitement kicks in and reminds me of why I began my journey.

But as Seneca the Roman philosopher once said:

> *'When a man does not know what harbour he is making for, no wind is the right wind.'*

> Seneca

Therefore, may this book help you identify, call out and reduce the bullshit in your life. And may it also assist you pick the right winds to take you to *your* harbour. Whatever, and wherever *you* define that to be.

Chapter 2

In the Beginning – My Own (Bullshit) Self-Discovery

My Personal Relationship with Bullshit

Let me begin by first giving some background on my own personal journey of bullshit self-discovery.

As a young adult I experienced several pivotal moments that clearly conveyed where a life filled with self-delusional habits, a lack of self-awareness, and listening to misinformation would take me.

It was a path I didn't want. But poor choices, poor habits, and a healthy dose of personally created bullshit, almost left me with no other options.

'Unless you are Planning on Getting a Brain Transplant, I Wouldn't Bother!'

These charming words were said to me as a 19-year-old when I was trying to work out my place in the world. I was grappling with massive uncertainty about a career choice. What was I suited to? Where could I be successful and happy?

Some context.

In my last years of high school, I was not the most motivated nor focused student. In fact, my amazingly ordinary study efforts continued well into my first years of university. To be completely honest, I was an extremely crappy student with a black belt in the art of procrastination. I lacked both focus and motivation, but above all, I was lazy.

I knew I wanted a career that would make a difference. A career that would give me satisfaction and fulfilment. But I lacked focus. Of course, I was still toying with my childhood dreams of astronaut or professional racing car driver. Unfortunately, I was fast realising my lack of endeavour would make both of those extremely difficult to achieve.

It was not until midway through my first year of university (a general science degree) that I finally decided on a career path. I was going to be a physiotherapist. Why not? I loved sport. And I loved the idea of helping people in need.

With newfound motivation and drive, I focused on getting the best marks possible. My plan was to transfer out of my general science degree at the end of the year and start my physiotherapist journey at another university. Simple! I didn't have anyone feeding me inspirational (bullshit) platitudes that I should 'just go for it,' or that 'I could be anything I wanted.' No. I was doing a great job of that myself.

When the end of the year arrived, my highly delusional version of hard work had, of course, resulted in a set of less-than-ordinary marks. 'Not to worry,' I told myself. 'The other university will fall in love with my clearly perceivable levels of maturity, and my enviable completion of the first year of my science degree.'

If only I could travel back in time and give myself a firm smack across the back of the head to wake my delusional self out of my self-deceptive ways. But never fear. Fortunately, I had someone else ready to do that for me.

I vividly remember my first interaction with the university that ran the physiotherapy program. I was certain beyond a shadow of a doubt they would be blown away by my "specialness" and immediately accept me, no *beg* me, to take up a place in their course. In fact, I was sure they would be *grateful* I had chosen them.

Brimming with confidence, I rang to confirm the application process. I was asked a few highly pertinent, but surely trivial, questions. 'What were your high school marks?' 'What were your first-year university marks?' I detailed my spectacularly ordinary academic history in all its glory. But what would it matter? I could be whatever I wanted to be, and I was going to be a physiotherapist.

I then heard the sentence that completely smashed my dreams and started my personal bullshit awakening: 'Unless you are planning on getting a brain transplant, I wouldn't bother.' Those words rang in my ears. I had no response. I had no comeback.

Calling Out My Own Bullshit

Of course, they were right. In that one sentence (so cruelly yet succinctly delivered), my dreams were shattered – and so too were many of my self-delusional habits. There was no way my underwhelming marks would ever have seen me accepted. Why didn't I recognise that myself?

It took me months to recover. My self-assuredness shattered, I deferred further studies and worked for a year in retail to clear my head and plan my next career step. It wasn't until after much soul searching and introspection, that I eventually decided on a different career path. I was now going to be a psychologist.

I decided I would resume my original science degree, but this time with a major in psychology. I had now realised I wanted to work in a profession that sought to unravel the complexity of human behaviour. A profession that focused on driving self-development, self-awareness and improvement. And clearly, these were all things that I too could benefit from. Why did I act the way I did? How could I manage myself so poorly? How could I be so unaware?

My Complete Bullshit Awakening

My personal journey of complete bullshit awakening was still another three years in the making. It wasn't until I finished my undergraduate degree that it fully transpired. Apparently, I needed an even bigger kick up the backside to finally make me stop my self-bullshitting ways and get real.

With my science degree in hand, and new-found drive and determination, I began submitting applications to numerous universities for a fourth year of study in psychology. Although my marks were still ordinary, I applied to the best course available, then the next best, and then the next. I was prepared to accept I might not get into one of Australia's *best* universities, but I was certain I would get into *a* university. Once again, I dreamt of being something, so of course, it was going to happen.

In total I applied to 14 universities. And how many rejections did I receive? 14 of course. Not one single university understood my dream or saw my potential. Not one! And that was the moment my personal bullshit completely caught up with me.

In an utterly dejected state of mind, I felt as though I had nothing. I had nowhere to study. I had a set of ordinary marks, no money in the bank, living with my parents, and now the very real prospect that my days at university were over. I would never be a psychologist. Completely and utterly devastated, this was the moment I finally realised it was time to accept the consequences of my lazy and procrastinating ways. To stop dreaming with my head in the clouds.

I can still recall sitting at my parents' home feeling shattered and humiliated. I had finally glimpsed what I wanted my future to look like, and now that future was underway without me on the other side of an enormous chasm I could not cross. A chasm of my own creation.

But I also remember the next twist in my bullshit journey with equal clarity. Mid-way through the first week of the new university year my lifeline arrived. One of the courses that had previously rejected me now had a space available.

It turned out I was the back-up, back-up to the *back-up* student should anyone not take up a position in the course. Luckily, several students had pulled out at the last minute, and another had pulled out right in the middle of the first week. To whomever that person is – I thank you. I owe you my career!

Freed of My Own Bullshit

All my bullshit had now been outed. I had stared straight down the barrel of where my self-deceptive ways were heading – and it was nowhere that I wanted to go. It was at that moment that I made a decision – I would no longer deceive myself. I would always face hard truths as best I could. I would strive to be conscious of the outcomes and ramifications of my actions. To understand and accept that what I do today, will have clear consequences on tomorrow – and the next day, and the day after that.

I embraced the new course. I embraced the learning. I embraced the opportunity. Not only my marks, but my mindset reflected a newfound focus and purpose. At a new university with new lecturers, I was able to reinvent myself. No one knew the old me. No one anticipated laziness and poor commitment. I was a blank slate, and I could rewrite my personal narrative.

I completed the course with outstanding marks, and a vastly improved perspective. But importantly, I now had the foundations in place to effectively call out my own bullshit.

The Name Says it All

The next 12 years quickly flew past. I travelled. I met my wife. I started a career. I even completed a Masters in Organisational Psychology.

But this time around applying for a course was a vastly different experience. Without bullshit and procrastination as my middle names, I applied for three courses. All three made me offers. With bullshit removed I had choices!

Then in 2007, I made the most significant decision of my career: to go it alone and start my own one-man consulting business. I had had enough of office politics and corporate ladders. Enough of dancing to the beat of someone else's drum. I quit my job, jumped off the corporate ladder and, just like that, *Bramwell Solutions* was born.

But it wasn't until I had launched myself into the market that something obvious and significant was pointed out to me: my chosen business name abbreviated to BS.

From a conscious decision-making perspective, this was completely unintentional. Ironic? Yes. Deliberate? No way!

But perhaps subconsciously, I was trying to tell myself something. Something that would guide me to where I find myself today. Writing a book about BS.

Without conscious intent, I had established a consulting business that was about building authenticity and trust, while directly and respectfully calling out bullshit. Bullshit behaviours. Bullshit work cultures. Bullshit communication habits. And most importantly, bullshit advice that I could see was driving people to heightened levels of stress, frustration and confusion.

I guess you could say I had literally created a bullshit business model by accident. Yet, one consistent piece of feedback I have received since launching *Bramwell Solutions* is that, despite my business name, I'm *not* full of bullshit. That is an honour I wear with pride.

Cutting out the Bullshit

Some of my motivators for self-employment were selfish and simple: I wanted to work from home, stop commuting, and ditch the corporate suit and tie. All the "important" things to consider when starting a new business.

But many motivators ran deep. I wanted to concentrate on making a genuine and tangible difference for others through my work. I had been in consulting roles where it felt as though the primary focus had been to achieve billable targets.

Therefore, I had been in roles where it felt as though I had sold services that wouldn't solve the problems they were intended to address. In short, I had sold bullshit. Given I was determined to rid my own life of rubbish, the last thing I wanted was to feed it to others.

I was determined to only provide services that I genuinely believed would be of benefit. Importantly, I would only offer services that the recipient genuinely needed and would gain value from.

Of course, not everyone knows when they need help, or what help they need. But I was clear my offering would be without a deceptive smoke and mirrors approach that offered baseless "magical pills of success."

I wanted to be in a position where I could truly connect with, and understand, my clients, and genuinely become a trusted advisor. I know that sounds like a cliché, but first seeking to understand before giving advice is a damn good starting point when building trust.

Once I had my brand, my image and my service offering sorted, I wrote down the core goals that would underpin my drive and focus. Goals that were significant to me. Goals that would give me true satisfaction and personal pride to reach. Goals that *I* determined, and that *I* set.

These were the goals that would help me create the life that I wanted. A life I could genuinely feel proud of.

Doing What is Right – Not What Sells

And so, since 2007 I have been *Bramwell Solutions*.

I have survived a global financial crisis, the joys of the arrival of my two children, and the many ebbs and flows of self-employment in between. I continue to be incredibly privileged to work with many amazing and wonderful people and organisations.

Naturally, there have been moments when I worried about my next project. But no matter what, I have focused on being true to my personal goals and values. I have remained firmly focused on doing what is right, not on what sells. To always tell someone what they needed to hear.

Sticking to this path has had its challenges. Most of us will happily listen to positive statements – 'You are the best.' 'You can be anything you want.' 'You can earn a seven-figure salary.' The simple fact is these statements sell. And they sell incredibly well.

Not as many want to hear practical and realistic advice – 'Hey, life can suck.' 'Try as hard as you want, but you may not get there.' They don't inspire. They don't fill us with self-belief or a drive to succeed.

But, importantly, these comments don't feed us with false expectations and bullshit.

*We have created so much bullshit we prefer to
hear, it is drowning out the truths we need to hear.*

Therefore, a significant objective that guides my work is helping others find the right balance between these two messages: the inspirational and the realistic.

Ideas that inspire and support us, while not creating unrealistic expectations and impossible goals that fill our heads with destructive bullshit.

What is the cost of sticking to an overly optimistic rhetoric at the expense of some cold hard facts and reality checks? What is it doing to our workplaces, our families and even our environment? A biased and unbalanced focus on believing we can be 'anything we want' drives the creation of societies, organisations and individuals that are purely focused on *more*.

To *have* more, *get* more and *be* more becomes the goal. Anything *less* than more is considered a failure. This is not a healthy balance. It is a destructive balance that must be challenged in order to find sustainable approaches that result in less stress, less perceptions of failure, and less perceptions of inadequacy.

Instead, we must have in place a healthy mindset that is created by having in place appropriately challenging, but achievable, goals and expectations. The result – personally rewarding outcomes and reduced stress.

Chapter 3

The Growth of Bullshit

The Disastrous Consequences

We are surrounded by negative symptoms of bullshit advice and a focus on *more*.

Our environment is being destroyed by our consumption-focused ways. We are personally being worn down by increased levels of stress and anxiety caused by unrelenting messages that tell us to aim higher and higher, for more and more.

In 2019, Australia alone recorded appalling numbers of suicide and suicide attempts. Each and every day, around 200 Australians attempted suicide. On average, eight were successful. And the trend is only heading up. The Australian Institute of Health and Welfare (AIHW) reported that from 2016-2018 the leading cause of death in Australia for males aged 15-44 was suicide. Further, AIHW reported that in 2017-2018, 13% or 2.4 million Australians aged 18 and over were experiencing high or very high levels of psychological distress.

The reasons behind these numbers are complex and numerous, and many are well outside the scope of this book, (and my expertise) to address. But from where I stand, bullshit advice and a strong focus on *more* simply can't be positive factors.

Misleading and manipulative advice is running rife. Outrageous expectations and increasing stress levels are the result. Therefore, it is without doubt, that these excessive expectations and stress levels must be contributing factors to the reported levels of psychological distress.

The reality is that, at times, life does indeed suck. And you know what? We can't all be 'anything we want.' I know that sounds harsh, but considered from a purely statistical perspective, not everyone can be successful if success is only defined as reaching the absolute top – the pinnacle of our field.

There are these annoying little things in the world of statistics called bell curves and distributions. No matter what, someone will be at the bottom, someone will be in the middle, and someone will be at the top. It is statistically impossible for everyone to be at the top.

A *Bullshit Distribution* narrative leads us to believe we can *all* be at the top, and we can *all* be whatever we want. Striving for anything less is presented as a failure.

But we can't all finish first. The collective average performance level will only shift up as everyone strives to be the absolute best. We don't all get to suddenly reach the pinnacle. No matter how good, the second best remains the second best, the third best the third, and so on. It is impossible for everyone to be the best. The impact on our self-esteem is disastrous if we have been erroneously led to believe that finishing anywhere other than first is a failure.

Time for a Reality Check

The outcome of the *Bullshit Distribution* narrative is the *Stress Distribution*. This is where an increasing proportion of individuals feel they are a failure for not being the best. And the harder they try, the pinnacle that defines successes remains out of reach.

Imagine climbing Mount Everest. Clearly a significant feat. But now imagine climbing the same mountain while it is still forming and pushing upward. With every step forward, the pinnacle shifts ever higher. This is what a process of excessive bullshit expectation and goal setting drives – attempting to reach a summit that, for many, is forever out of their grasp.

We must see and accept that being in a location *other* than the top is not a failure. There are so many other measures of success and happiness: the journey, the learnings, attempts to improve, the enjoyment of what we do achieve, and accepting and embracing ourselves as the unique individuals we are.

But the way we create and set our goals is shifting away from the beneficial outcomes of learning, expanding, and evolving. Instead, our goals are increasingly focused on the end outcome alone. And what is that? *More* of course!

In the past, we would inspire ourselves with statements such as 'I'm going to give it my best shot.' 'I'm going to leave no stone unturned.' 'I'm going to work at being the best.' Fast forward to now, and these statements have been replaced by 'I *will be* the best.' 'I *will be* successful.' 'I *will be* whatever I want.'

The first set of statements were fundamentally different. Even if we didn't reach the top, we could reflect on and learn from the journey. Getting there was not the sole focus, it was the icing on the cake.

The German author and statesman Johann Wolfgang von Goethe wrote:

'By seeking and blundering we learn.'

Johann Wolfgang von Goethe

It was about valuing the process of *'seeking and blundering'* to learn. But the second set of statements have changed the equation. Now, for many, getting there is everything. It is less so about self-discovery and self-reflection, and more about succeeding.

And, if we are not successful? We then move too quickly to negative self-criticism. 'I failed.' 'I didn't try hard enough.' From this negative mindset, it is only a short hop, skip and jump to an 'I *am* a failure' mentality.

It is this pressure; and it is this resulting mentality, that creates a greater risk that many will not reach their expected level of performance. The bar has been set at a personally unattainable height. Perhaps unattainable due to a fundamental lack of core skills or abilities needed to succeed. Perhaps due to a lack of self-awareness to understand the personal development required. Perhaps due to forces completely beyond our control – a lack of opportunity or a lack of resources.

This is where the disastrous impact on self-esteem, self-worth and mental health is manifesting into record levels of depression, anxiety and so incredibly sadly – suicide. We are buckling under the weight of expectation – our own expectations and the expectations of others.

We too frequently lack an objective perspective to recognise and appreciate the other victories that exist – the journey, the learning, the growth. We lack the objective perspective to spot bullshit that serves only to create pressure. Bullshit that is counterproductive to supporting positive and healthy self-appreciation.

It's Obviously Not New

The amount of bullshit in our lives is on the increase. While the concept of bullshit is nothing new, its form is changing and its impact increasingly insidious.

Once bullshit was merely bragging about supposed accomplishments or claiming grandiose achievements and successes that were hard to challenge or discredit. Our exaggerations and lies were often no more than slightly annoying fabrications. Fabrications presented as an attempt to make the messenger appear more attractive and knowledgeable. They were often embedded in well-intentioned beliefs or outdated thinking.

Now, it is far more toxic. These exaggerations are being dressed up, rebranded and sold as "expert" advice. Opinions emerge from a self-selecting few who claim they, and *they alone*, know the truth at the heart of an issue. "Success gurus" create ridiculous expectations that cause many to pursue stressful, illogical and unattainable goals, and dead-end career paths. We are pushed to achieve our wildest dreams. In fact, we are even coaxed to perceive our dreams as not being wild enough.

Compounding this, our ability to critically evaluate and assess the validity and veracity of information appears to be rapidly diminishing. Poor advice and ridiculous expectation setting are running rampant. We have become so focused on *being* more, *having* more and *succeeding* more, that we are too frequently neglecting to check the facts of what we are sold before we buy.

As a result, our ability to question and constructively differentiate fact from fiction means we are susceptible to allowing bullshit advice to govern and define who we are. Too many are far too easily deceived by the smoke and mirrors of the fast talker, while ignoring contradictory hard facts. For too many, this represents a fundamental flaw in our logic and critical thinking.

We must take action to stop drowning under the stress created by this fixation on achieving and having more. Unfortunately, the increased stress and expectation that we place on ourselves is reinforced by a plethora of social media commentary and "expert" advice. Much of this advice is self-serving, short-term focused and bullshit. It has no balance nor substance. Is there consideration of the long-term implications? Is there consideration of the bigger picture perspective? Do we stop and consider the needs of others? Or are we being enticed to focus solely on satisfying our own needs and goals?

I'm by no means suggesting we are *all* falling into a singular, self-centred pursuit of our own needs. But my concern is that too many of us are – and without realising it. The collateral damage of this pursuit will be felt by many. Those who are pushed aside, those told to aim higher and higher, and those who face an ever-raising bar of expectation to jump over.

The Evolution of a Self-Centred Focus

I recall an opinion I heard in the late 1980s about the evolution of a self-centred focus. It was observed that during the 1960s and 70s university students protested wars and rallied against apartheid. They championed freedom and fairness for all. By contrast the students of the late 80s (of which I am one) protested student fee increases and the high cost of alcohol at the campus bar.

The 80s students were seen as only championing causes that were related to their own personal circumstances, self-interests and self-concerns. It was a harsh generalisation (and certainly not true of all students), but to me it resonated as a powerful insight into how our cultures and interactions were potentially shifting at the time. If we were shifting away from a focus on improving the rights of others, then what would be in its place? A selfish, self-serving *me, me, me* complex?

This is where bullshit advice has jumped right in and been festering and growing ever since. Advice that has propagated and emboldened an excessive focus on the pursuit of personal goals, personal success, and achieving more. The mantra of 'if you can dream it, then it is yours for the taking' was born, and it has been growing unchecked since.

Working with large corporate organisations has shown me that an overly biased focus on self-centred needs is certainly very much alive and kicking in our corporate worlds as well as in our private life. From the board room to the mail room, from strategic meetings to informal chats at the water cooler, from the sports field to the playground – it has too frequently become all about *me*.

Day in and day out we can witness, and may even be involved in, interactions where self-esteem and pride are lost and taken, in which respect and trust are trampled on and diminished. We may approach our interactions with positive intent, but if we are excessively focused on our own personal needs, we too often lack the skills, self-control, and motivation to start and finish interactions in a respectful and long-term focused manner. Despite our thousands of years of evolution and development it is the 'fight-or-flight' behaviours that are all too often easier to deliver and easier to ingrain. They are natural responses that are focused on the preservation of self.

By contrast, it is the intelligent and empathetic responses that are the hardest to execute and sustain. These are the types of behaviours that underpin collaborative interactions. Interactions that are less self-focused, and less driven by ridiculous expectations and poor advice. But it is these empathetic responses that are under threat from a self-centred focus.

Excessively Self-Centred Pictures

Even the way we record and hold onto our most cherished moments is becoming infused with a bullshit self-centred viewpoint. In the past our photos catalogued our lives. Our photos helped us hold on to memories, accomplishments and significant moments. The happy moments and the memorable moments. The memories and moments we wanted to share with our children, and our children's children.

They were moments we wanted to reflect on and remind ourselves of the joy we felt, the outcome we achieved, or perhaps a time we savoured with a friend. Significant points in a relationship, or wonderful shared memories with friends and family in locations that we wanted never to forget. It was frequently about what was around us – the setting, the event, the *people*.

I look back at my photos from my younger years and can often remember exactly what I was thinking. One of my most cherished photos is of my wife in Prague taken many years ago. We had only been together a few months, and I was madly in love. She was Danish, I Australian. We had met in London and were travelling Europe together. The obstacles to a long-term relationship were blindingly obvious. The likelihood that our relationship would go nowhere was high.

But I look at that picture and I can remember with absolute clarity what I was thinking at the time: 'I'm going to marry this girl.' Now 25 years on, several moves from one side of the world to the other, and two children later, we are still very happily married. For me, that picture will always represent that beginning.

But look at the world now. Where are the pictures that will catalogue our lives and capture moments to pass on to future generations? Many of our photos are no longer about the setting, the event and the people. The focus is now on the individual. The 'selfie' has taken over.

According to Google statistics, an estimated 93 million selfies are taken per day globally on Android devices alone. It's estimated one third of all photos taken by people aged 18 to 24 are selfies. 'Look at ten photos of me from near identical angles pouting in a favourite top.'

Worse still, one study even found that globally over 250 people died between 2011 and 2017 while pursuing the perfect selfie. 'Here is the last picture of Mark standing precariously on the edge of a cliff!' But what is the point of this type of picture? Millions of images where the beautiful scenery is just a nice back drop, as opposed to being key to the moment? What do they convey about our self-worth, and our self-esteem? Have they simply become another means by which our self-interest fixation manifests?

I've seen countless photos of breathtaking views, with a person in the foreground striking a contrived "perfect pose" or "perfect look" – the sole aim to achieve social media likes and shares. But why travel to an exotic location if the primary goal is to take a picture to share? Why not simply buy a large poster of that amazing location, stick it on a wall, do your downward dog yoga pose in front of it, and then take the picture. Same effect. Much easier and cheaper to achieve!

But this self-centred fixation is taking an even uglier turn – we are falling into a trap of self-loathing for not looking like catwalk models in our own pictures. Despairingly, even our expectations of physical appearance are succumbing to the *Bullshit Distribution* and *Stress Distribution* narratives – to be the "prettiest," "coolest" or even the most "daring" – hence the 250 deaths.

The number of Apps available to distort our appearance are numerous. Apps to accentuate our eyes, to remove the slightest perceived imperfection to present flawless and radiant skin, shining hair, and a sparkle in our eyes – literally. Apps that insert ridiculous bunny ears sprouting from our head, and a cute little black spot on the end of our nose.

This morphing and filtering of images has become so widespread and toxic that the term 'Snapchat Dysmorphia' has been coined to encapsulate the growing tendency of the young and impressionable to be deeply dissatisfied with their personal appearance. Those with low self-esteem wish for their actual physical appearance to resemble what is created by the morphing App filters – unnaturally large eyes, impossibly narrow checks and waist, and unrealistically flawless skin.

I struggle to understand the thinking behind some of these images. But I can definitely imagine future conversations between parent and child remembering past generations. '...and this is a picture of your great grandmother trying to look like Bambi.' Yep, that will certainly create a lasting memory.

Once photos were about sharing memories and resharing experiences. Now, for too many, they represent self-obsession, insecurities and capturing acts of selfishness.

Oh, how the language of our photos has changed.

Spotting and Rejecting the Toxic Bullshit

We must become better skilled at identifying and removing the bullshit from our lives. To recognise the messages and rhetoric that will only lead to a stress-inducing pursuit of more. Spotting the advice from "experts" that we would be all the better for ignoring and shying away from.

I recently read the promotional spiel for a workshop that promised to teach the opposite of this book – how to successfully focus on getting "*more.*" The spiel commenced with a huge declaration that the number one thing everyone in the world wants is MORE! It then listed all that could be had. More success, more happiness, more passion, more money, and more productivity. All in abundance, and all to be initiated from a single one-hour workshop.

But it is this type of advice that will surely be most successful at creating shallow, materialistic, and stress-inducing life goals. Goals that will send us down an exhausting path in their pursuit as we are pushed to find a "higher level" of performance to "have it all." This advice, this type of "inspirational" messaging, is destructive on so many levels. To be challenged to aspire for so much more in unrealistic amounts, and in unrealistic timeframes. To strive for stress-inducing levels of performance that may well be forever unattainable.

For what happens if we can't reach this "higher level"? Sure, this type of hyperbole may encourage some to remove obstacles and realise improved outcomes. To remove obstacles such as apathy and procrastination.

But what about the individual who is already at their "highest level"? What of the individual who is now striving ever harder for an unattainable state of being? What of the individual who is already stretched to the limit of their physical, mental, and emotional capability? What of those whose current measure of success is being able to hold it all together for another day. Then trying to hold it all together for the next day, and the next?

This promotional spiel captures my concerns in a nutshell. A relentless focus on more, and less so on enjoying the process of learning and the attempt of something new. Being led to believe that we can all reach that ever-higher level and be whatever we want if we just imagine it.

But if this pursuit doesn't give us more? Then what? Does that mean we must have failed somewhere along the line? For many of us, the most significant impact of this type of messaging will not be growth. It may be varying levels of wasted time and resources. It may be messages that fail to inspire and have no lasting impact.

But for some, it *will* be the deepening of feelings of inadequacy, stress, and failure.

> *This stress-inducing merry-go-round ride founded on the setting of unrealistic expectations and pressures must stop.*

It is time to get off and find another ride that will support and enable a truly balanced and successful life. Balance and success that we determine according to *our own* specific situation, needs and aspirations.

Part 2: Identifying and Removing the Bullshit

Understanding how bullshit advice and expectations have woven themselves into everyday life to create an obsessive focus on more, stress-inducing pursuits, incomplete self-awareness, and poor communication practices.

Chapter 4

When Enough is No Longer Enough

A Massive Bullshit Driver

Before reading on, consider that chapter heading again.

'When enough is *no longer* enough.' It's a ridiculous statement. How can enough *not be* enough? By its definition, enough refers to the existence of the required amount. For the required amount or expectation to have been met and satisfied.

How can it *not be* enough? Because enough is increasingly no longer the desired amount. In both our work and personal lives, we are shifting to a stress-inducing position where for something to be considered *enough*, it must now actually be *more*. To *provide more* than what was asked for. To *give more* than what was initially expected. To *be more* than we previously dreamt of. As a result, we have created this non-sensical position where *enough is no longer enough*. Unchecked, it could go even further to where enough will *never* be enough.

A singular pursuit and expectation of *more* is dangerous. Dangerous to our self-esteem (will we ever truly experience and bask in the sunlight of success and satisfaction?). Dangerous to our sense of self-worth (are we ever contributing enough, if enough must always be more?). And dangerous to a world that doesn't have inexhaustible and infinite resources (is it even possible for us all to have more to the level we demand?).

The Pursuit of More

This relentless pursuit of more is exhausting. And one day it must surely be exhausted.

We are surrounded by messages that tell us we don't have enough, that we haven't achieved enough. We are bombarded with advice to aim higher and go further. Where merely doing enough, and not going further, is seen as indicating a lack of innovation and creativity.

We are urged to constantly push our boundaries and step outside our comfort zone. We are urged to feel inspired and pursue ever greater dreams while adhering to the mantra of 'you can be whatever you want to be.'

No longer can a child dream of being a racing car driver (as I once did). No. They must aim higher. They must be more creative. Why be the driver when you could own the whole damn team? Emblazon the car with your name – *Bramwell Racing*. Start a new competition and conquer the world as an innovative start up that uses a yet-to-be discovered energy source to power the cars. Use social media to spew forth a constant stream of imagery and commentary for others to see and hear just how *special and successful you are*.

Ok, maybe I got carried away there. But you get my drift. Yet, this is exactly what is happening. We are constantly being sold the message to 'aim for the stars.' And if we are not aiming high enough, a relentless bombardment of senseless motivational statements will keep pushing us to aim higher.

This is something I'm going to specifically call bullshit on in Chapter 12.

But who then is left to do all the other stuff? The necessary stuff that, if no one does it, all this dream chasing will come to nothing? If we are all aiming incredibly high, who amongst us will have everyday realistic expectations?

Who will be safe, predictable and reliable in their everyday work and life? Who will be the "doers" if we all have our heads in the clouds trying to out-innovate and out-create each other?

The expectation is just too much.

The Impact on Praise

The sad reality is that this pursuit of more has even created a situation where we no longer reward an individual for doing what is required. These types of people are now known by the negative phrase of 'just doing their job' or 'just doing enough.' Instead, we heap praise on those that go above and beyond and do *more* than what was expected. But isn't it confusing? Stop and think about it: if you only do what you are required to do, that is no longer deemed good enough.

What happens next? If we motivate everyone to go the extra mile, then at some point this extra mile will also become part of 'just doing their job.' Must the expectation then become an extra, *extra* mile? And so, on it goes. A perpetual cycle of pursuing more and more and *more*.

The greater and greater demand placed on our physical and intellectual capabilities and resources is exhausting and draining. At some point, somewhere along the journey, something must give. Either we break this cycle of ever-increasing demand, or it will break us.

Surely doing enough, should still be precisely that: *enough?* We need to stop striving for the extra mile and the extra effort in absolutely *everything* we do. We need to embrace and value things in life other than the relentless pursuit of *more*. To embrace the simple fact that, for many of us, doing *enough* is exactly what should be expected – and for some, it is all there is to give.

We must shift our pursuit away from always working to get more and achieve more by first enjoying and placing greater valuing on what we already have – to celebrate and cherish what we have already accomplished. I recently read an article about the creation of new organisations in our modern global economy. In it, a particular comment jumped out at me:

> *'Everyone celebrates the "start-ups," but no one celebrates the "keep goings."'*

We celebrate all the new and shiny things, but we fail to place as much significance on something that remains steady and continuous. We have created such an obsession with having more and more, that we are at a point where even the continuation of something that already exists is regarded as mundane and boring. The demand is for constant innovation and growth.

How is this sustainable, or even achievable?

The External Impact

What of the impact on our external environment? Our workplaces? Our communities? And broader still – our ecosystem?

Governments around the world are looking to reduce their carbon footprint, to change our poor environmental and consumption-focused lifestyles to be in tune with the realisation of how fragile our eco-system is. An ever-increasing number of countries and their peoples are realising we can't sustain our current habits.

But far too often we apply a time discount to the impact of poor behaviours and the consequences of destructive actions. 'Don't worry about that it's a long way off.' 'That won't happen in *my* lifetime.' These are troubling and toxic mindsets. Well, guess what? The impact of these mindsets is here now.

Pollution levels are escalating at an alarming rate. Holes in the ozone layer are growing. Global warming has become the greatest threat to mankind. If a self-serving pursuit of our own interests is not soon tempered with a balanced, long-term and comprehensive understanding of the impact of such a myopic focus, then eventually there will be nothing left. Zip. Zero. Zilch. Just a dead, uninhabitable planet and only our stressed-out selves to thank.

While there may be small shifts in our goal hungry approach driven by the threat to our eco-system, evidence is continuing to pile mountainously high as to the dire impact of global warming. This threat is driving a growing and strengthening shift toward a recognition that humanity must live in a manner that is more sustainable and harmonious with our environment. A recognition that without this shift, a global climate disaster awaits.

We need to reduce our wasteful and unsustainable footprint on our planet. Right now!

> *We must stop stomping around, leaving bigger*
> *and bigger footprints to show how important we*
> *are. We need to instead walk more softly.*

The Internal Impact

And the impact on ourselves? Why can we no longer be happy with what we have? What is the impact of a strengthened self-centred mindset on our psychological well-being?

The signs of the internal impact are exceptionally concerning. As commented earlier, suicide rates are on the rise. Mental health disorders are running rife. We are increasingly stressed and exhausted juggling work, personal, and family expectations.

Too many are all too happy to swallow the 'more' rhetoric that is pushed down their throats by savvy marketing organisations, and a plethora of experts who will 'help us get there,' – wherever 'there' may be. We must halt the promoted perspective that it is a failure or weakness to not pursue more. The modern-day marketing message that relentlessly pushes us to consume must be countered.

The industry of 'more' is massive, sexy, and very appealing. Who would not want more?

I once saw a goals board promoted by a life coach on social media. An actual physical board that was to be placed in a prominent, and highly visible, location in the home or office. The board was to then be covered with images and statements to create a visual representation of an individual's goals and aspirations. A constant 'in your face' reminder of what was to be achieved. A constant motivator to not give in, give up, or be distracted from your goals.

To help, the life coach provided an image of their personal board. It showed pictures of a luxury car, a cruise ship, a diamond ring, and countless other materialistic aims. Not one single image suggested the giving of a single thing. Not one thing that would suggest improving the life of another human being. Nothing at all.

Every single image on the board was focused on expanding material possessions, or in engaging in high-cost and luxury pleasure activities. Please don't get me wrong – I'm *NOT* anti-fun. I too like nice cars and holidays at beach resorts. But this board promoted nothing but self-interest and personal gain. All get. No give.

How can this be healthy and sustainable? How does it add value to our community and environment? How does it help create a balanced and healthy life?

The Explosion of 'Imposter Syndrome'

The pressure created by a life forever focused on striving for more is not healthy. And a constant feeling of enough no longer being enough is disastrous for some.

One specific negative outcome produced by excessive feelings of inadequacy for not delivering enough, providing enough or even *being* enough can be the creation of an *Imposter Syndrome*. Here, sufferers feel as though they are a fraud – doubting whether their skills, abilities and experiences are sufficient to justify the role they occupy, or the responsibilities they manage.

A debilitating mindset is created that constantly questions and second guesses decisions made, and actions taken – doubt creeps in and undermines self-belief.

Levels of trust in personal capability and competence dimmish as they compare themselves to others who appear to have it all and achieve it all. Feelings of inferiority flourish, and a downward negative spiral ensues.

The default is a position of sustained and intense self-doubt, coupled with a fear of being exposed as seriously deficient in the knowledge and skills needed to perform effectively. Bottom line – our dysfunctional relationship with the concept of *enough no longer being enough* seriously risks causing an erosion of our self-confidence and self-belief.

Without a more balanced perspective, the prevalence of an *Imposter Syndrome* will only escalate. Effectively shifting this mindset to a more positive outlook is almost insurmountable when messages abound that enough must be more.

A recalibration is urgently needed.

Chapter 5

The Alternative - Recalibrate: "Enough is Enough"

The Need to Reset

We need to reset. Reset our goals. Reset our focus. Reset our persistent desire for more.

My hope, my wish, is that a reset will give us the opportunity to pick an alternative path that is richer. Richer with empathy. Richer with compassion. Richer with trust. Richer with authenticity, sustainability, and connection. Surely a message that tells us to enjoy what we have, be more giving and supportive to others, and to stop the blind pursuit of more, should be a popular one? But to hear it, we must first stop listening to the constant push for more, and the abundance of ensuing bullshit messages.

We too often perceive that we are judged by the amount and quality of our possessions: judged by the impression we leave and the impact we have. But what if instead of focusing on possessions and impressions, we focused on creating sustainable societies, and healthier environments in our work, home and personal lives? What if we also measured our worth by what we *give*, not just by what we *take* and *use*? Imagine if the majority measured success by how they enriched not only their own lives, but the lives of others for the better.

We need to take this message and translate it into all our life habits. Yes, use fewer plastic bags that are harmful to our precious environment, but also make it personal. Stop being driven by bullshit advice and bullshit expectations that make it hard to step away from the bullshit pursuit of more.

I started calling out bullshit years ago. Is it time for you to now do the same?

> *We must clean up the pollution in both our external environment and our own internal headspace.*

A Goals Reassessment

The following quote by the entrepreneur E. Joseph Cossman is often promoted as a positive motivator to help us remain focused on the successful achievement of our goals:

> *'Obstacles are things a person sees when he takes his eyes off his goal.'*
>
> E. Joseph Cossman

But what if, by taking our eyes off our goals, we realised the goals were wrong, or in urgent need of review? Might we not see other richer alternatives?

At the very least, there is surely value to be had in periodically sitting back to pause. To lift our head and cast our gaze about to determine if there is something else to be had in life beyond the goals we are currently pursuing. To reassess their relevance. To recognise that what Cossman called 'obstacles,' may in fact indicate the existence of new goals that are better alternatives. Higher order for ourselves, our society, or perhaps even our eco-system.

Perhaps they are 'obstacles' that present significant shifts in our environment to necessitate and enable a substantial rethink of life as we have structured it.

The year 2020 will be remembered as the year of the COVID-19 pandemic. The resonating impact on our way of life will be formidable and, I'm certain, unforgettable.

But it is a devasting 'obstacle' that also presents opportunity. An opportunity to step back from the path we have been pushed to relentlessly pursue. To step back from the daily grind of modern life, and question how we have structured and managed our existence.

It has presented an opportunity to reassess many of our daily routines and habits. To reassess how our time is allocated to different components of our life – to challenge the need to commute for hours every day to an office. Time that could be better spent with family or friends.

The impact of COVID-19 will also hopefully include a reassessment of what has been pushed upon us by "experts" who tell us rampant consumerism and self-obsessed behaviours are the norm. To reassess the merit of those who tell us 'you must put yourself first, because no one else will.' Well of course we must if everyone else is taking on board that same poor advice.

To consider how our lives can be better balanced and structured to reduce unnecessary stress and develop a greater appreciation of non-material things – family, friendships, and wellbeing.

Author, poet and humanitarian Sonya Renee Taylor captured both the devastating impact of COVID-19 and the opportunities it presented humanity when she said:

> *'We will not go back to normal. Normal never was. Our pre-corona existence was not normal other than we normalised greed, inequity, exhaustion, depletion, extraction, disconnection, confusion, rage, hoarding, hate and lack. We should not long to return my friends. We are being given the opportunity to stitch a new garment. One that fits all of humanity and nature.'*
>
> Sonya Renee Taylor

I have read that COVID-19 is seen by some as nature hitting back: telling us that we need to change our ways.

If it is, then we need to listen.

Identify the Bullshit

The impact of a constant stream of high expectations, 'aiming for the stars' and being told that we can be anything we want is stressful. The message that we are failing if we don't realise our full and complete potential is exhausting.

Undoubtably, one of the greatest learnings I gained from both my upbringing, and my days at university, was the skill of critical thinking. Constructively challenging ideas and concepts to assess their validity and relevance. But sadly, as I have already mentioned, our ability to think critically, to analyse and assess information based solely on its merits, is on the decline for many. Perhaps it has been lost somewhere between the void of counting our social media impressions and watching cat videos on YouTube?

Whatever the cause, this decline in critical thinking in turn impedes our ability to challenge these exhausting messages, and to recognise that aiming so high, and for so long, is self-destructive bullshit that will not end well. We need to rediscover the skill of critical analysis to remove bullshit from our lives.

So where do we begin?

A first step is to constructively identify all the pieces of bullshit that exist. Pieces that are in plain view. Pieces that need to be unearthed. Pieces that, if removed, will change our life for the better. We must focus on self-improvement. Identifying what battles need to be outwardly fought, and those that must be inwardly fought. What requires a constructive stand? What requires a subtle internal shift?

Are the expectations that we place on ourselves (and others) realistic? Are they balanced? What behaviours should we change? Should we stop listening to that "self-help guru" others have sworn by? Should we directly, but sensitively, call out a behaviour, or even the lack of a behaviour, we find destructive and thoughtless?

We need to encourage and support people to feel comfortable in their own skin and their own abilities – to lessen the weight of expectations that we are burdened with. We need to focus on enjoying this precious life that we have.

Removing Feelings of 'Imposter Syndrome'

In its entirety, this book provides skills and perspectives to remove this counter-productive thought pattern. But below are a number of specific questions to promote immediate self-reflection – to challenge this negative mindset and help "clean up" your headspace.

Do you excessively fixate on negatives? Do you excessively focus on what has yet to be achieved while ignoring past successes and accomplishments? Do you hear and respond to feedback received in a balanced manner – or do you discredit and downplay positives, while focusing in on, and magnifying, negatives? Even then, are the negatives truly negative, or viewed from a warped or distorted perspective that catastrophises small points for development, into major points for poor self-criticism?

Answer these questions honestly. Use the content of this book to help define relevant and realistic goals and expectations. Refine your self-awareness to understand and appreciate your true skills and abilities more accurately. Then couple this with a fair and accurate understanding of how others perceive you. And importantly, ensure your focus is balanced between where you are heading, with where you have come from. Balanced between what is *yet to be* learnt and accomplished, with what *has already been* learnt and accomplished.

Calling out Bullshit

It is time to call out and remove unwanted stress and needless crap from our lives – to call out advice that leads to poor interactions and decisions. But to achieve this we must become better skilled at challenging the bullshit we both see and hear.

It is time to start a bullshit calling movement where we reject the pursuit of *more*. Where we reject and challenge messages that drive self-centred and narrow-minded decision-making and selfish behaviours. To combat this, and promote balance, we must call 'Bullshit!'

Calling something out as bullshit includes challenging advice that has negatively impacted different aspects of our life. Perhaps our work-life balance, our leadership style, our communication techniques, or another of the multitude of components that comprise our existence. We must challenge advice that is proffered by "experts" – some of whom lack the skill, ability, proven success, or even relevant base-level education in the area they claim expertise.

We need to educate and empower a greater number of people to call bullshit on senseless rubbish. To no longer feel that 'just doing enough' is wrong. To encourage leaders to value, support and praise team members that *are* doing enough. To stop always expecting something extra as the default position and better appreciate those who give exactly what is required.

In short, we need to start the *That's Bullshit Movement*.

So next time you hear something that sounds ridiculous, unrealistic, and farfetched: call it out. It doesn't have to be a loudly shouted 'BULLSHIT!' (I don't want to get people fired or damage personal relationships). Instead, it could be an internalised, but confident rejection. It may be a well-articulated and assertive push back, or it may simply be a knowing nod, followed by a decision to hit the ignore button and move on.

But remember: the focus of calling out a behaviour or opinion should never be to hurt, harm or belittle others. Nor should those outcomes be acceptable collateral damage.

Why? Because that would be bullshit too!

We must challenge unrealistic expectations about how we must live – to be aiming higher and higher to achieve perfection in all we do.

The 'More Shift'

This is most definitely not about driving a culture of pessimism or laziness. It is about driving and fostering a critical assessment of the 'more' orientated mantra.

So much of our orientation and relationship with the word 'more' is *toward* ourselves. We want to be more and have more. We seek more pay, more possessions, more success, and more status.

But look at each of those wants. Each is associated with *getting* and *having*.

What then do I mean by the 'More Shift'?

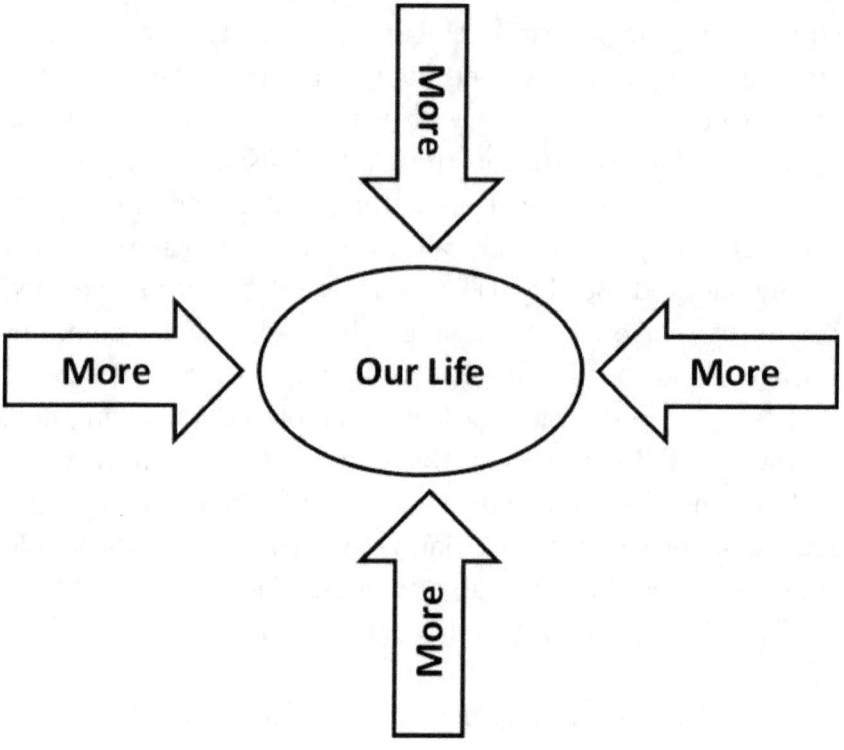

Instead of solely focusing on *getting* and *having* more, we need to shift the orientation and relationship with the word 'more' to also include an outward focus. A focus that also encompasses enriching others, and, by association, enriching ourselves.

Doing so, removes an excessive fixation on high stress-inducing pursuits of more, as we instead also strive to give more, help more, and mentor more. Notice how the word 'more' now comes second in those statements.

The focus now includes meaningful actions that improve our lives *and* the lives of others, rather than just 'more for me.'

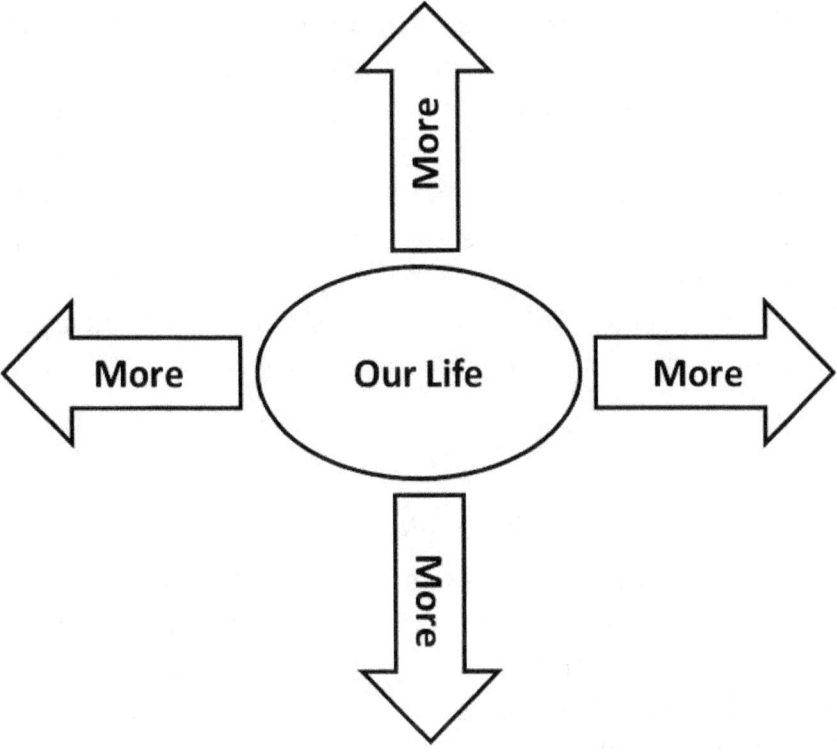

But, once again, there is much bullshit that needs to be challenged to achieve this shift. I'm not suggesting we forgo all our worldly possessions and live in a commune growing organic vegetables and singing Kumbaya in bare feet (although if that is your thing, go for it!).

But consider this; how can we be a truly inspirational leader if our primary pursuits are to earn more, have more and climb that corporate ladder? How can we achieve work-life balance if our focus is on striving to achieve and get more in every aspect of our life? How do we balance being an amazing parent, keeping fit and lean, eating the perfect foods, getting that pay rise, killing that project, being in the high-performer development program at work, and a super star in sports?

It's Bullshit.

How can this be sustained? Something will eventually break. And that something could well be you.

And then who is going to pick up the pieces? Our family and friends who are also likely struggling under the same pressures? Our colleagues who are on the same bullshit pursuit treadmill? Our boss who is balancing between managing up, down, and all around? Our sporting teammates who are aiming to play at an elite level, which means showing how much better they are than everyone else in their team?

Again... Bullshit!

Reassessing Your Relationship with 'More'

A good starting point to commence the 'More Shift' is to reflect on what you have determined to be important pursuits in your life. To comprehensively review your relationship with 'more.' Therefore, the following is a simple two-step activity to help get you thinking about your current goals and drivers.

1. Identify the Drivers

First, identify your stress drivers. To do this, you must reflect on all the facets of your life – work, home, family, friends, hobbies, sports etc. Consider all the different key components and review each separately.

What information have you been fed to drive your behaviours at work? What are you seeking to achieve at home? Do you know what is, or is not, constructive or destructive in your life?

Now make a list. Write down the key words of advice and ideas that helped create the way you have chosen to live your life. Is it an approach that still suits who you are today? Is it an approach that will support who you aspire to be tomorrow?

2. Determine the Impact

Second, consider how each of these pieces of advice have impacted your life, your relationships and your decisions. Do they add value to you? Do they add value to others? Then determine whether there are contradictions between the different facets of your life. Advice for success in one facet, that will undermine and damage another.

Use this self-reflection to prioritise what needs to be called out and addressed first. Where is the bullshit in your life? Even if you carry minimal bullshit, this 2-step process is a healthy way by which to revisit and recalibrate your drivers and goals on a regular basis. Remember:

Achieving self-awareness is a journey, not a destination.

So, let the journey begin.

Chapter 6

Self-Obsession is not Self-Awareness

Are You Self-aware?

The achievement of true self-awareness is powerful.

Understanding how we are perceived by others, understanding how we react to given situations and people, and understanding our triggers and behaviours enables us to manage our emotional reactions, communications and relationships effectively.

Further, a strong and accurate sense of self is critical for setting realistic and appropriate goals. Goals set with accurate self-awareness are formulated based on a true understanding of our strengths, weakness areas and potential capability. This contrasts with setting goals based on an inaccurate sense of self, and an over inflated ego fostered by poor advice, such as the good old 'aim for the stars' mentality.

However, self-obsession is *not* self-awareness.

Many claim to be self-aware when in fact, they are not. Research undertaken by the Eurich Group reveals the full extent of this self-awareness blind spot. Their research has consistently found that, although most people report *being* self-aware, only 10-15% of people they studied actually *were*.

But how can such self-awareness blind spots exist when so much time, energy and money is invested into personal growth via a massive global self-help industry? In 2017, the Global Wellness Institute estimated the wellness industry to be worth over $4 trillion US dollars globally, with growth of over 10% per year. Within this, it was also estimated over $600 billion US dollars was spent on fitness & mind-body development alone.

Have we then always been this delusional and inaccurate in our self-awareness, or is our modern way of life, and the impact of this massive self-help industry actually destroying self-awareness and instead driving self-obsession? Are we becoming blind to how the world impacts us, as well as our impact on it?

The Eurich Group's work also proposed two distinct components of self-awareness:

- **Internal** – an awareness of who we are and what we want
- **External** – knowing how others perceive us and understanding our impact on others.

Considering this distinction between internal and external awareness, it appears the primary focus of the self-help industry's attention has been on strengthening our internal awareness, while neglecting our external awareness.

Building our understanding of internal awareness is only half of the self-awareness equation. Therefore, merely focusing on improving our internal awareness is how too many have stepped on to a path of self-obsession instead of self-enlightenment. Advice that solely fixates on prompting an understanding who we are is both misleading and incomplete.

Therefore, missing from the self-awareness development mix is the key ingredient of external awareness. It's this critical ingredient that shifts self-obsession to true self-awareness. Balancing internal reflection with an external perspective that focuses on understanding how we are perceived by others, ensures that we don't become self-centred and self-absorbed.

Drawing on both an internal and external awareness creates a deeper sense of self as we balance the realisation of our own needs with critical consideration of the needs of others. Only with such a balance can we then demonstrate true empathy and compassion. Empathy and compassion that is also founded on a sharply focused awareness of how achieving our own personal goals will impact others – for better or for worse.

Poor levels of self-awareness are also driven by warped internal and external self-perceptions. From an internal perspective, there is a plethora of advice about how we should define our goals and aspirations. There is a constant monologue in our ears of how great we are, and that 'we can be whatever we want to be.'

Over time, this constant feed of biased bullshit causes a distorted self-perception. From an external perspective, our self-obsession and distorted egos blind us to what others really think of us, and how we impact them.

The outcome is an unrealistic expectation and idea of what we think we want, value and can achieve. It is too frequently based on "expert" advice – and frequently by "experts" who know nothing (or little) about our life circumstances. We create an inflated positive perception of our ability and potential, while lacking a healthy dose of reality checking.

Understanding Your Impact

To modify, develop and improve our interactions with others, it's critical we comprehensively understand how our communications and mindset impact our surroundings. We need to understand how we truly respond and react to our environment. And we need to achieve a level of insightful self-awareness that genuinely supports effective personal development.

As a first step in this journey of self-development, we must better understand the consequences of our behaviours. This first step is vital. If we don't at least attempt to consider the true impact and consequences of our behaviours on others, then we lack a central ingredient necessary for the level of self-awareness needed to support personal development.

We need to fully understand and comprehend why our interactions and communications succeed or fail. We need to recognise the personal brand that we have created, and fully understand its impact and effect.

Without such a review of our communication consequences, how does a poor communicator recognise the need for change? We need to identify where change is required, and then understand how instances of poor communication may negatively impact our interactions – from the simplest to most complex.

Without such self-reflection, it would be easy to suggest that attempts to change our behaviours are shallow and disingenuous bullshit. Superficial change only pursued for selfish gains – to make our lives easier, or to allow us to manipulate others to realise our own wants and desires.

Technology Enabled Selfishness

The positive impact of technology on our productivity is obvious. What is less obvious is the negative impact of technology in diluting our self-awareness. This is particularly true of social media platforms.

It is here that self-obsession is constantly mistaken for self-awareness.

Many of the emerging mediums of communication provide an even greater degree of separation from our audience. Technology provides a vast physical distance between the person making comments, and the target of their commentary. The result is diminished accountability.

Technology has emboldened us to make harsh judgements, hurtful comments and give stinging criticism, while hiding behind anonymity. There is a perceived arm's length to our comments, and therefore, a deterioration of our levels of ownership and responsibility for our actions and remarks.

We are far more willing to make negative and critical comments of others when using emails, as opposed to when speaking face to face. While emails may facilitate frank and pointed dialogue, we are becoming adept at using emails to express opinions without due consideration of their impact – both immediately and long-term. Do we stop to evaluate whether our opinion is considerate or helpful? Whether it is counterproductive or destructive? A 'who cares you deal with it' communication style is easy to deploy when we can't see the impact or long-term consequences. All these processes and mindsets work to undermine the notion of building true self-awareness.

The disintegration of self-awareness, and a lack of ownership of both our remarks and actions, is consequently disastrous. Without these skills and traits, we limit our ability to effectively socialise, develop, grow, and flourish as positive contributors to our societies. As remarked by the theoretical physicist, Albert Einstein:

> *'I fear the day that technology will surpass our human interaction. The world will have a generation of idiots.'*

Albert Einstein

The Impact of Technology on Personal Growth

In the mid-20th century, Swiss psychologist Jean Piaget studied the stages of a child's cognitive development. Piaget proposed children progress through four distinct stages: from basic thinking, to concrete thinking, through to complex and abstract thinking. Piaget's final stage of development was the *Formal Operational Stage* – the ability to *think about thinking*.

With Piaget's theory in mind, consider our obsession with technology. Is this obsession hindering our advancement to Piaget's highest level of cognitive ability? Is this obsession creating an obstacle to reaching the *Formal Operational Stage* by drawing us into hours of online game play and staring at computer screens? This is time spent on activities that reduce the frequency, and quantity, of meaningful interpersonal interactions. Interactions that require active self-monitoring, self-reflection, and an awareness of our impact on others in order to learn and evolve our interpersonal skills.

If this is the impact of technology, then consequently it should be expected there would be a negative impact on the attainment of true self-awareness. We would be less effective at constructively thinking about, and reviewing, our own behaviours and intentions. A quick look at social media certainly brings up an abundance of childish and irrelevant bullshit posted by far too many adults – if you genuinely think anyone really wants to see a picture of what you are about to eat, and the after-you-ate empty plate shot, then you truly *are* seriously lacking external self-awareness.

I have also lost count of the number of headshots I have seen posted on social media espousing the value of achieving self-awareness. They are usually accompanied by a statement proclaiming that we must 'learn to love ourselves before we can love others.' That we must 'know who we are before we can know others' etc. Yet, ironically, many of these images are highly filtered and edited to make the poster look younger, thinner, taller and "smarter." How does such editing reinforce the need to love yourself first? How is offering manipulated images to look "more attractive" (another bullshit concept) a form of genuine self-love?

Such images sadden me greatly and reinforce the extent to which true self-awareness is lacking.

Our "Interaction Rights"

Individuality – and the right to be able to choose our own paths and direction in life – is a central right of every member of a free and modern society. Although not free from consequences, we are essentially free to choose. But we must balance these desires to exercise our own "rights" and 'be whatever we want to be' with the needs of our society, and the groups and organisations to which we belong. And, of course, our families.

This balance is needed to ensure the way we interact, communicate, and influence is not always solely driven by the pursuit of our own needs and wants. We need to consider the external perspective of self-awareness when choosing what actions and behaviours we choose to demonstrate.

Consider what could be termed our "interaction rights." I'm not referring to basic human rights such as access to shelter, clean water, and an education, but rather our processes of communication.

These "rights" include actions such as:

- Refusing requests without feeling guilty
- Seeing our own needs as important as the needs of others
- Expressing ourselves freely (without purposeful intent to hurt)
- Changing our minds as we see fit

- Not knowing and not caring to know
- Pursuing our own interests as more important than the interests of others.

At first read these seem fair. The consensus being that these are all "rights" that we should all be free to exercise. However, cracks appear when we pause to consider what daily life would be like if these were exercised liberally. Blindly, and without restriction, applying these "rights" would promote an outcome of every person for themselves. All our actions would be based on our own best interests. Life would be a constant series of battles and conflicts in which we each seek to win and preserve our own rights above the rights of others.

A world where we all liberally exercise our "interaction rights" as a priority, is not a world that I would wish to be a part of. However, this is precisely what so much of the self-help and motivation industries push. The *'me, me, me'* focus and mindset. A biased weighting to the development of internal self-awareness at the cost of external self-awareness.

While we are not at a point of complete self-absorption and self-interest, there are many worrying signs that this is the path many are heading down. We can't solely blame technology and social media platforms alone for the degeneration of values and morals. They are merely the vehicles, the enablers, that are allowing us to revert to caveman-like behaviours in which the laws of the wild hold sway. Each person to fend for themselves, and a 'look after number one' mindset, as no one else will.

Compromising to Find Balance

I recall an occasion at the end of a workshop when a participant informed me they were displeased with the content I had presented. The workshop challenged participants to develop the necessary skills to communicate their views and opinions in a manner that was both constructive and outcome focused.

The participant perceived himself to be an introverted and introspective thinker who was extremely sensitive and caring in his approach. He felt it was unfair for me to set an expectation that such an introverted person should communicate his opinions in the workplace, even when a situation warranted it.

But this is yet another danger of poor self-awareness – where we use our supposed self-awareness as an excuse to justify inaction and resist change. Some use it to empower excessive action, while others use it to allow themselves to be walked over. The development of self-awareness should be an empowering and insightful process that assists us determine how to best respond and support ourselves to identify and address specific skill gaps. But too many appear to use self-awareness in a dysfunctional way. A better balance is clearly needed.

It is not only the extroverted and domineering types who must recognise the need to moderate their approach and temper how they exercise their "interaction rights." So too the reserved and introverted must constructively push themselves to express key opinions and challenge the status quo when warranted. If not, the domineering shall domineer, and the introverts will exercise their right to withdraw. Such a mix can't be good.

Therefore, we must *all* be willing to compromise our "interaction rights." We must recognise the moments to step forward in our communications, as well as the moments to step back and hold our tongues. This can only be achieved with the support of accurate self-awareness and genuine self-insight.

But we must also be astute at recognising the benefits our interactions provide us. This will allow us to recognise when we are reinforcing resistance and building obstacles, and when we are removing blockers and motivating others to respond to our requests. We need to alter our behaviours to suit the broader needs of our community, organisations, sporting teams and families. We need to achieve a complete picture of self-awareness by being both internally and externally self-aware – only then can we to make the shift from self-obsession to self-awareness.

Chapter 7

The Alternative - The Beginnings of Self-Awareness

Holding Up a Mirror

Our starting point for balanced self-development must include detailed clarity of the here and now.

We must think about what we *are*, what we *are not*, and what we *seek* to achieve in our interactions and communications. How we desire to be regarded – both by ourselves and by others.

Success in achieving substantial and sustainable self-development is not based on how good or bad our beginning point for self-development may be. It is about the degree of accuracy we have – how well we understand who we truly are, and who we truly aren't, *right now*.

How we are perceived by others *right now*.

To do this, we must consider our responses to questions such as:

- What are our strengths?
- What are our weaknesses?
- In what situations do we struggle?
- What are our buttons that can be pushed to illicit a poor response?
- With what personality types do we struggle?
- What are our fear-based responses?
- What are our overly confident responses?
- What are our biases – both conscious and unconscious?

Answering these questions accurately, and with sufficient detail, is neither an easy or quick process. It can be confronting. It takes much self-reflection.

This self-reflection needs honest and constructive self-feedback, balanced with frank feedback from others. But once we have constructed a detailed profile of who we are, we can work further to better understand how we are perceived.

Only then can we be in a far stronger position of knowledge to correctly identify specific improvement needs, and undertake a focused, targeted, and authentic process of complete self-development – from an internal *and* external perspective.

Once this self-insight has been constructed, we must review and evaluate our behaviours, our skills, our strengths, our weaknesses. We must determine and define what would be both aspirational and realistic goals to pursue. Goals free of cheesy and stress-inducing bullshit.

We must identify and magnify those behaviours that are positive and constructive, while we identify and remove those behaviours that are excessively self-serving and destructive.

8 Key Questions for Self-Reflection

Below are eight key questions to support balanced self-reflection. Each question covers a specific point that is crucial for developing a strong foundation for self-awareness. Each question challenges us to deeply consider the intent and consequences of our actions. To become more focused on our cause-and-effect considerations to best understand how we communicate throughout life.

It is not possible to pause and consider our response to each question before every single action and decision point encountered. However, by evaluating our position against each, it is possible to better clarify who we are, and what we stand for. This will in turn facilitate a greater awareness of the consequences of our actions, and whether these consequences are acceptable, and truly aligned with our own values and beliefs.

Take time to pause and reflect on each.

1. What is the long-term perspective?

We typically engage in specific sets of behaviours, and approach situations in a particular way. Therefore, it is critical to periodically take a moment to step back and assume a long-term perspective. We need to understand how our future will be impacted by what we say and do now.

Will a short-term gain be at a long-term cost? Will immediate negative consequences be minimal, but magnify over a sustained period and snowball into something greater? Will immediate reactions fester into far greater concerns, with an impact far beyond what was intended?

By taking a long-term perspective we are better able to see both the bigger picture and the consequences of our current behaviours. What may seem like a drop in the ocean now, with a broader and long-term view, may be revealed as having significant potential for a negative ripple effect. A growing long-term negative impact on our future interactions.

Consider: *Short-term gains are not worth long-term losses.*

2. Are we aware of our emotional reactions?

Do we fully comprehend, value – or even consider – the emotional responses associated with the different behaviours we engage in?

Take for example, conflict avoidance. While this strategy may make us feel safe and free from confrontation, it may also allow our own negative emotions, as well as the negative emotions of others, to fester and solidify. Eventually, this can cause a volcano-like eruption to release built-up stress, or, worse still, detrimental health effects from anxiety levels pent up within.

Alternatively, venting and yelling may see the target of our aggression simply give in. But will they now be an ally willing to help in the future? Or will they only provide the bare minimum of support and input to avoid our anger again?

We must avoid interactions that create silent assassins, those who are scheming behind our backs to undermine our work, while fearful of further conflict or a future verbal berating.

We must be skilled at identifying and removing instances where our emotional 'fight-or-flight' mechanisms determine our course of action. These types of protective and defensive emotional reactions must be removed.

In their place must be emotions that support the effective evaluation of relevant information to illicit a calm, considered and astute response.

Consider: *Know the emotions that drive a response.*

3. Have we considered alternative positions?

It can be easy to become so engrossed in the positions we assume, and the intricacies of a situation, that we over-play our own interests and concerns. The result is a neglect of other's needs.

We must always be aware that our actions *will* impact others; be it positive or negative. The way we manage these impacts will speak volumes about who we are. To consider alternative positions also challenges us to evaluate the credibility and relevance of the perspective we have adopted. It also forces greater consideration of factors connected to developing external self-awareness.

Too many times I have worked with leaders who continue to persist with a specific approach or solution to an issue. A fresh perspective would immediately reveal that this "tried and true" approach is in fact failing dismally. How often do we hear the justification 'this is the way we have always done it'?

Thoughtful consideration of alternative perspectives and positions helps create a continuous improvement mindset. It helps us to avoid getting stuck in ruts, or short-sighted thinking and poor problem-solving patterns.

Consider: *There is always more than one perspective.*

4. What are we trying to achieve?

Being passionate about topics, and becoming engrossed in our interactions, are strengths to nurture and reward. But like all good things, too much can be dangerous.

Becoming overly engrossed and blindly passionate can cause us to neglect viable alternatives, as well as the valuable contributions of others. At its most extreme, we lose sight of our initial objectives. We get so caught up in the interaction that the desired end outcome is overlooked or lost.

It is critical to keep at the fore of our thinking the notion of what we want to achieve. Consider this when working through negotiations, picking our way through complex conversations, and traversing a multitude of interactions.

It is important to not lose sight of our destination. To do so can result in poor habits: arguing for the sake of arguing, or striving to demonstrate superiority, greater intellect or manipulation skills.

These poor approaches are excellent for achieving selfish outcomes – but even better at burning bridges, laying down poor groundwork for long-term relationships, and destroying respect. In short, we may feel we have achieved something productive, but again the long-term negative consequences may far outweigh any gains our victories achieve.

Consider: *Keep the end destination in mind.*

5. What are our values?

Are we truly aware of our values? For our own inner values to effectively guide our behaviours, it is not enough to simply claim to be a moral person with high values. What does a statement like that even mean? It's similar to a company that develops its organisational values, and then expects behavioural compliance by sticking the values up on every available wall space throughout their office. Typically, such organisational values are developed with little (or no) consultation with the staff they aim to hold accountable.

The result is poor values connection, and no meaningful identification with what the values stand for. Further, merely stating the values on a laminated card at reception doesn't mean that they are automatically adhered to, understood, or have any influence on behaviour whatsoever.

We must not make the same mistakes with our personal values. Don't compose a set of meaningless and trite personal values that we simply "laminate" and place in the front of our mind.

With little self-reflection it is easy to declare lofty values. Values that we pull out like a calling card when we assume a moral position, defend an action, or reinforce a denial.

We must honestly reflect on whether our values have *genuinely* been developed to guide moral and honourable behaviours. Or have they been pieced together as a group of ingratiatory behaviours to seek creditability and favour with others?

Too often when people are asked why they live, or seek to live, by a given set of values, they struggle to clearly articulate the why. Perhaps they were passed on to them by a previous generation? Perhaps they sounded good? Perhaps it has simply been concluded that being without values is undesirable?

We must take time to reflect on our values. We must make strong and clear connections to the tangible behaviours and actions that would, and would not, exist if we were adhering to these values in all aspects of our life.

We need to review our current behaviours. Are we acting in a manner that is truly values aligned?

Consider: *Know your values inside out.*

6. What would an observer perceive?

It is easy to become so immersed in a situation, so wrapped up and engrossed in the moment, that the expression 'can't see the forest for the trees' becomes very appropriate.

A useful exercise to prevent this from occurring is to take regular opportunities to step back from our actions and communications and assume the perspective of a third-party observer. Considering what others may observe helps us identify when we are losing perspective, and perhaps, becoming too emotionally involved and losing objectivity.

This method of stepping back out of a situation is like pulling our head out of the sand, where in this instance, the sand is the interaction. I have personally found this approach to be incredibly effective. It has assisted me time and again to recognise, in both my personal and professional life, when I have crossed over the line from being tenacious to obnoxious. Unfortunately, hindsight has also shown me that I have at times waited far too long before taking this important step back.

This poses a predicament: if we are so obsessed and absorbed in an interaction, will we be capable of pausing to prise our head out of the sand? It takes effort, but I guarantee practicing this perspective shift will prove its worth ten-fold. If we are aware of our personal tendencies, then over time this will become a natural component of our communication repertoire. Further, it will also become an essential reflective habit that will greatly assist in strengthening external self-awareness.

Consider: *Don't stand too close to the trees.*

7. Is it sustainable?

A key aspect of assuming a long-term perspective is to also consider whether specific behaviours are sustainable. If the answer is no, then this may be an indicator that the behaviour in question is inappropriate, and that it is a symptom of a self-awareness blind spot. Consider a specific behaviour you currently display:

- Does it have adverse psychological or physiological effects on you?
- Does it have adverse effects on others?

For example, in the heat of the moment, 'fight-or-flight' responses can feel rewarding or protective. But if these reactions become our *modus operandi*, then the negative impacts can be substantial.

It is critical to recognise that sustained 'fight' mechanisms of anger, abuse, or the aggressive projection of emotions, will only serve to alienate and offend those around us. Sure, we may feel that our point has been made. But if we continue to do so in this manner, then eventually we will have no one left to make our point to.

Conversely, 'flight' responses that put our needs below the needs of others, by not expressing and dealing with our emotions and uncertainties, may, as already mentioned, help us to avoid conflicts. They can help us avoid being placed in situations that may make us feel uncomfortable and vulnerable.

But sustained behaviours of this type can also result in low self-esteem and issues of poor self-worth. Opportunities are missed to table our thoughts and ideas.

It's also ironic that people who constantly engage in 'flight' responses to avoid conflict, fail to realise that these avoidance behaviours too often result in highly emotional and confronting conflicts being delivered right to their doorstep. Instead of dealing with conflicts in their juvenile beginnings, strategies of avoidance and withdrawal can feed conflicts until they reach a fully-fledged adult state.

Adopting behaviours that deal with situations in a productive and positive manner is far more beneficial. This approach nurtures and develops our relationships and helps us to achieve a balanced and accurate self-esteem. It also heightens our levels of self-awareness through deeper insights and realisations made from facing issues and resolving differences.

Consider: *Focus on sustainable behaviours.*

8. Will the broader outcomes enrich?

Finally, it is extremely important to consider whether the reactions to our behaviours will generate positive outcomes.

Will they make us feel enriched and better as human beings? This may sound somewhat grand, but imagine a society where we primarily focused on engaging in behaviours that not only bettered us as individuals, but also produced productive and positive outcomes for our communities, organisations, families, and friends.

It's easy to fall into poor behaviours that provide short-term gratification. Behaviours that demonstrate no consideration of their impact on others. Behaviours that are counterproductive or unsustainable.

By contrast, we should be focusing on behaviours that produce rewarding outcomes for all. We should be building relationships that will be sustainable through the demonstration of behaviours that we can reflect on with self-satisfaction and pride.

To do so, we need a strong moral compass to negotiate our way through the maze of choices we must select from. The notion of a moral compass also allows us to continue to head in the *right* direction. It allows us to know where the right direction is, regardless of how our life terrain changes or what obstacles appear before us.

Sadly, we typically only hold a map in our hands as we select our paths to travel. We use a one-dimensional and static representation of life to respond to the myriad of problems, challenges and obstacles that are thrown before us.

A strong moral compass allows us to focus long-term *and* make decisions that are better grounded in our core beliefs and values.

A moral compass helps us avoid making decisions, and taking actions, that are short-sighted and based on shallow advice. It helps us avoid actions that are excessively biased towards our own personal needs.

Consider: *Focus on behaviours that enrich both ourselves and others.*

A Self-Assessment

Now bring all your self-reflection together. For each of the questions above, review your current behaviours and mindset. Make note of potential areas of contradiction or lack of defined clarity.

For each specific area, can you spot if you are carrying any bullshit? What has created this position? What current assumptions and learnings must you challenge to improve your self-awareness?

How can you create greater authenticity between who you are, and who you aspire to be?

Comprehensive and honest self-reflection takes time and sustained effort. Don't rush this process.

For as Benjamin Franklin once said:

> 'There are three things extremely hard: steel, a diamond, and to know one's self.'

Benjamin Franklin

A Reminder – Open your Eyes to Help

Self-awareness invites greater self-monitoring so that we can better avoid tunnel vision and a failure to see alternative paths. But sometimes we become so caught up in our own dramas and concerns that we fail to see the bigger picture. I was reminded of this one morning when driving my two children to school.

An accident had caused a major traffic gridlock ahead. The usual 2-minute school commute was now a 20-minute nightmare. As we sat going nowhere fast, a car ahead stalled. With cars backed up in all directions, and with frustration levels already extraordinarily high, tunnel vision kicked in for many drivers.

It was as if the broken-down car was suddenly draped in a cloak of invisibility. Drivers hunkered down and averted their gaze. They ignored the distressed driver of the broken-down vehicle as repeated attempts failed to restart the car.

Instead of offering help, drivers reverted to ridiculous and dangerous strategies to get passed. They drove over nature strips, curbs, and median dividers in the road – doing anything to avoid stopping to help someone clearly in a time of need. The easier option appeared to be choosing wrongs rather than choosing a clear right: stop and help.

Personally, I saw no other option. Central to my personal values is a focus on helping others in need, whenever possible, and whenever safe to do so.

So, I stopped. I reassured the distressed driver and waved down others to help push the car off the road. One of whom later thanked me for getting him to help; regretful someone else had needed to point out the obvious, and right thing, to do.

Ironically, those that did nothing barely moved forward in the gridlock. Was ignoring someone distressed and in need of assistance worth but a few metres?

Determining what is right is not always easy. Yet, in this situation I thought it was obvious. But given the behaviour of so many others – apparently not!

Ask yourself: Do you know what you would have done? Hunker down or help?

Chapter 8

The Misuse of Assertiveness

A Common Misperception

Behaviours that are focused on self-obsession rather than self-awareness promote communication techniques that are heavily biased towards achieving our own personal needs – to help us 'get what we want.'

This is where bullshit teachings of some self-proclaimed "communication experts" have taken the positive concept of assertive communication and caused it to be misunderstood, misrepresented, and incorrectly used.

Assertive communication was never intended to be about 'getting what we want.' This approach implies manipulation and aggressive overtones. Further, such a focus is devoid of empathy, fails to consider alternative viewpoints, and fails to understand the specific needs of those we are attempting to influence and direct. When approached in this manner, assertive communication does nothing but drive self-centred actions and support the pursuit of personal needs at the expense of others.

Assertiveness was originally created to assist individuals overcome high levels of anxiety. It was developed as a form of communication that included techniques and strategies to effectively express opinions and needs in a constructive way. It was focused on enabling communication to occur with less feelings of guilt or anxiety.

But unfortunately, over the ensuing decades, the concept has progressively morphed so that it is now often misunderstood, and incorrectly aligned with a twisted self-serving notion.

This is a classic example of bullshit. It takes a process that was designed to assist the vulnerable, the struggling, and the weaker communicator find their voice, and twists it to become a disingenuous process of manipulation. At its most extreme, it's even presented by some as a valid tool to pull out of our communication toolkit when we're not getting what we want. A way to take our communications up a self-serving level.

It's More than Being "Direct" and "Honest"

Poor versions of assertiveness are frequently demonstrated by the levels of directness and honesty conveyed. Effective assertiveness does indeed include these two ingredients, but it is the amount and intent of the two that are frequently skewed to a level of overuse and a self-serving bias. It is the skewed overuse of these two components that facilitates the proliferation of an approach that excessively places personal needs before the needs of others.

The direct and honest components of assertiveness were not intended to empower the communicator to say whatever they felt like, whenever they felt like it, to whomever they felt like. But unfortunately, this misperception has strengthened over time. It is where the bullshit sales pitch steps in and presents assertiveness as the vehicle to empower you to 'get what we want, when we want it.' 'Come learn how to get *more* of what you want' becomes the tag line.

No, instead the direct and honest components are about promoting frank, open and constructive dialogue. Again, the concept was to support the individual lacking in confidence and self-esteem to feel comfortable directly conveying their opinion with greater honesty and openness. As opposed to indirectly conveying opinions with the hope they would be heard, or lying to oneself that we were comfortable with a situation, when in fact we weren't. Therefore, a central premise of assertive communication was based on building the confidence to express a constructive opinion, and to not self-deceive.

However, I have learnt the hard way how easy it is for a direct and honest approach to be morphed into a force for evil rather than good. Many years ago, I ran an assertive communication workshop where I used the terms of directness and honesty to help define assertive communication. At the completion of the session a participant, who had been timid and withdrawn at the beginning, pulled me aside to convey how deeply the workshop had resonated.

It had hit home. Changes to personal communication style were now to be made. Self-deceptive ways would be challenged. No longer would there be a pretense of happiness if it didn't genuinely exist. The workshop had helped this individual find their voice. Opinions would now be confidently expressed. As a facilitator, this is what you live for: to have a significant positive impact on the lives of others. I remember feeling exceptionally proud of this outcome.

Months later when I again ran the same workshop, two participants discretely approached me before the session to introduce themselves as colleagues of the participant who had found their voice in my previous workshop. I readied myself to hear of the amazing progress made. I anticipated glowing feedback of how the previous participant's extreme positive behavioural shift had inspired these two to attend my next session – to realise equivalent enlightenment.

What they described was the complete opposite. They were indeed attending the workshop on the recommendation of someone, just not from the source I expected. Instead, they informed me I that had in fact created a monster. I listened on as they proceeded to describe how the previous participant's newfound voice was that of a tyrant.

Honesty and directness were being used to let everyone within ear shot know exactly what was thought of them. 'You annoy me.' 'You're lazy.' 'Your quality of work is substandard.' This was the voice I had empowered. This was the voice of someone expressing their unbridled honesty and directness. Apparently, this was the voice that had been aching to come out, and this was the voice I helped unleash.

I had assumed that within the context of the workshop materials the terms 'honest' and 'direct' would be correctly interpreted and understood as forces for good not evil. I learnt two valuable lessons from this experience. Never make assumptions about the clarity of your message, and always be crystal clear.

So, in all assertive communication workshops since, I now ensure participants understand that:

> *Assertiveness includes being honest and direct –*
> *about what's relevant, in a constructive manner,*
> *that does no harm.*

Challenging Communication Bullshit

When assertive communication is used in a dysfunctional manner, there are typically several phrases and statements that must be challenged. Phrases and statements that masquerade as attempts at assertiveness, but are really nothing more than attempts to empower a person to do wrong. They are attempts to rationalise or intellectualise crude and offensive statements that are aligned with the notion of 'getting my own way' or 'doing whatever I want' to satisfy personal needs.

The following examples are some of the most notable excuses used to justify poor communication strategies. If you are guilty of any of these, now is the time to stop and hold that self-awareness mirror up for closer inspection.

1. I must yell to be heard

This is a communication position typically used by individuals who lack the skills to push their point of view forward, respectfully and constructively, when met with resistance. They have adopted the belief that some situations justify yelling, screaming, and getting in someone's face to convey a point of view. These are viewed as totally acceptable behaviours.

Worse still, they consider yelling and screaming to be a logical final step in any good and well-structured conflict resolution process.

The perpetrator of this communication strategy starts out soft, pushes harder when they feel their point is not getting across, and then when needed, launches into full yelling mode to achieve their desired outcome. Unfortunately, those most skilled at this approach often decide to save time and proceed straight to the yelling stage. Why even bother with the softer initial steps?

Poor self-awareness, and poor consideration of the negative impact on others, is supported by subsequent selective observation and listening. These 'yellers' only take notice of when the approach supposedly "worked." They ignore all symptoms of how it failed: fear, animosity, and lack of trust and support, to name but a few.

This approach is a perfect example of closed thinking. It doesn't push the individual to develop healthy communication and influencing skills. It serves only to get one's own way, but with immeasurable negative costs, that may not always be immediately apparent. There are devastating costs that may take days, weeks or even years to materialise. But eventually, the destruction of trust, respect and collaboration will catch up.

The truly skilled and self-aware communicator should never, at any point in any interaction, resort to yelling and screaming. As a last resort walk away. Let it go and return when cooler heads can prevail.

Bottom line: *If you must yell to be heard, it is a communication failure.*

2. You can't teach an "old dog" new tricks

Making changes to our communication style and mindset is no easy task. If we have been communicating in ways that are poorly considered and executed for years, or even decades, it is unrealistic to embark on a journey of change and expect to reach our destination overnight. It will take a long-term commitment of practice, adjustment, and self-reflection. Creating and *sustaining* excellent communication skills is a life-long journey.

It is akin to gaining maturity. We can all learn and adapt to some degree, but to do this we must be able to identify the why and what, and then be willing to accept the need.

Having recognised the magnitude of the task before us, we must be committed to continuing our journey of self-development. Unfortunately, too many who are unwilling to challenge themselves, or others, are fearful of what critical self-reflection may bring to the surface.

Of course, there are also those who are simply too lazy to try. So far, they have managed to falter through life relatively unscathed. So why not leave well enough alone? For these individuals, it can indicate unrealised potential.

Whatever the driver, the mindset of 'you can't teach an old dog new tricks' is just plain bullshit. It's a poor excuse to not try.

We can all learn and make changes for the better, irrespective of our background, experiences, abilities, personality, upbringing, age or gender.

Granted, key factors such as our personality profile, our education, and our support network will make it easier (or substantially harder) to change. But if we have the right motivators, the right objectives, the right goals to aim for, then anyone is capable of pursuing and achieving positive improvement.

The key is to find what will excite and motivate the "old dog" so that tangible benefits can be perceived from improving and changing ways. It may be factors such as increased self-respect, or an attempt to please significant others. The challenge is to find the right motivators and set in place the right communication objectives that will genuinely excite.

If you are a leader of people, how can you excite and engage a team member? If you are a parent, how can you excite and engage a child? If you are a sports coach, how can you excite and engage a player?

There is no easy solution. It takes careful planning and execution.

Bottom line: *We must connect with others according to their specific motivators and drivers.*

3. It didn't hurt me

Another counter-productive view is 'if something didn't hurt *me*, then it won't hurt *you*'. This is driven by the narrow-minded belief that if the individual survived a poor experience, or feels adversity made them stronger, then others should also be made stronger by the same experience.

One common way this plays out is in the perpetuation of poor leadership. There is a wealth of research to demonstrate the positive impact praise and recognition has on employee engagement and performance. Despite this, far too many leaders continue to adopt the same inadequate leadership and communication styles of their past leaders and managers.

Inadequate styles that lack the delivery of genuine and authentic praise and recognition. The current leader feels the past environments they experienced helped make them the "success" they are today. They replicate this past environment in their own behaviours, irrespective of the reactions of current team members and peers.

Of particular concern is the number of poor leaders who become executive coaches, spreading their bullshit to others as some secret formula to success. Rather than break the chain of poor communication and sub-standard leadership, these so-called coaches perpetuate bullshit. Thereby, ensuring the next link in the chain of poor leadership is formed.

The difficulty here is opening these people's eyes, and get them to see that:

- A 'one size fits all' approach doesn't apply
- What worked for one, may be completely counterproductive to another
- Their definition of success is fundamentally flawed, as it does not take into consideration whether the true potential of their followers has been realised.

We each need to evaluate our actions openly and honestly. We need to identify if we are perpetuating any chains of substandard behaviour. We need to identify what superior behaviours can be formulated and honed instead.

Bottom line: *It absolutely can hurt others.*

4. I don't mean to be rude, but...

This statement, and a thousand variations like it, are far too frequently used to present opinions that are exceptionally narrow in their thinking: thinking that lacks insightfulness and understanding. These qualifying remarks are a means to justify a closed mindset. To claim no ill-meaning if offence is taken by the statement, and to absolve responsibility for any hurt or distress caused.

Any statement that starts 'I'm not trying to be difficult, but...' typically means we are about to be. Starting with 'I'm not a racist, but...' typically means a short-sighted racist statement, based on mass generalisation and lack of knowledge, is about to follow.

These statements put the listener immediately on the defensive. The listener is now waiting to hear how we will prove in our words, actions and tone that we are *exactly* what we claim not to be. Removing these statements helps to remove excuses from our dialogue. Removing the initial qualifier means the communicator must better consider whether their statements are in fact inappropriate.

These qualifiers can be used to justify actions that are self-serving, indicate a biased mindset, or closed thinking.

The examples are numerous:

- 'I don't mean to interrupt, *but...*' (I will anyway)
- 'I don't think my needs are more important than yours, *but...*' (I think they are)

- 'It's not that I have made up my mind already, *but...*'
(I have made up my mind)
- 'I don't mean to be blunt, but... (prepare yourself for an onslaught).

Another point to challenge in these statements is the use of the word 'but.' I've had many coaching and training participants tell me of how they have been advised not to use 'but statements.' Some have even been told to avoid using the word 'but' completely.

I can only partially agree with this. My partial agreement is because an overuse of the word 'but' can indicate defensive or turn-waiting listening. These methods of listening are commonly used when we listen only to hear what will allow us to push back and defend our own predetermined position. They can also be used when we are not listening at all – when we are simply waiting until the other person finishes so that we can then have our turn.

Neither approaches are appropriate. Both should be avoided.

My disagreement with the avoidance of the word 'but' altogether is because the word itself is not the problem. It's not the word that conveys a poor position of listening or lack of consideration. It's the bullshit that precedes and follows it.

Removing 'but' from our dialogue, without removing dysfunctional habits, only results in a different word being used. 'I don't mean to be rude, *but...*' now simply changes to 'I don't mean to be rude, *however...*' Same stink, simply different words.

Bottom line: *It is not the words that stink, it is the concept behind them.*

A Reminder – You Can Teach an "Old Dog"

Often a person who refuses to learn and change their ways first needs to better appreciate the full scope of their impact on others. Next, they need to appreciate the full range of benefits that change will provide. Only then will genuine behaviour change be possible.

Many years ago, I had an exceptionally frank conversation with a training participant. He was an older gentleman who was approaching retirement. He had the reputation of being an intimidating and bullying communicator. If someone didn't agree with his point of view or his abrupt style, he had a few standard responses: 'Build a bridge and get over it.' 'Go eat some concrete and harden up.'

The brief I received was that he needed to attend a public assertive communication workshop to learn how to better engage and communicate with his colleagues. To communicate in a respectful manner.

Unfortunately, his position as a content-matter expert made him indispensable to the family-owned business, but the breaking point had been reached when he reduced the CEO's own daughter to tears with his harsh and belligerent approach.

His participation in the day-long workshop commenced as would be expected. Arms crossed, frown on face, and minimal participation. But a change began as he listened to others explain how behaviours from their own colleagues, with similar approaches to his, had left them feeling deeply hurt and belittled.

As we worked through a review of what assertive behaviour is and is not, I could see subtle changes appear in his body language and participation. He started asking questions in the small group discussions. He asked others how it felt when someone treated them in a demeaning manner. What was said that was so hurtful? He leaned in and listened intently to the responses.

When we stopped for lunch, he approached me privately away from the group. He looked at me earnestly, and in a lowered tone said:

'I'm beginning to realise I'm a prick.'

His remark has stayed with me to this day. It will always remind me why I love what I do: that change is always achievable. Achievable even for those who demonstrate extremely poor and long-term entrenched behaviours.

I must admit that it was not what I expected to hear. We discussed what this revelation meant, and how to translate it into positive behaviour change.

The smile on his face was also truly memorable.

Chapter 9

The Alternative - Modern Assertiveness

Recalibrating – Modern Assertiveness

It's time to recalibrate the concept of assertiveness back to a force for good, rather than a force for manipulation.

We need to return assertiveness to its original intent – to support improved positive communications. But we need to modernise the initial concept to create and embed a version of assertive communication that is applicable and beneficial to all. A version that can underpin *all* communications.

I call this *Modern Assertiveness*.

The original clinically founded version of assertiveness was a communication process to use when feeling threatened or uncertain. It was designed to be used when confidence to deal with specific situations or people was lacking. *Modern Assertiveness*, by contrast, can be a way of life to help rid bullshit communication practices, and replace them with empathetic and constructive alternatives.

Modern Assertiveness is about how to best present opinions, ideas and concerns while focused on achieving the best possible outcome – for all, not just self. It's a communication style that accepts that getting what *we* want, may not always be the *best possible* outcome. Therefore, it also includes a preparedness to recognise that what was initially regarded as the best possible outcome, may prove to be incorrect when we assertively listen and question to fully understand an entire perspective or situation.

It is about having the communication skills and self-confidence to accept that our initial view was seen through the lens of our own preconceived perspective. To then have the confidence and comfort to readily change our opinion should it be necessitated by the introduction of new information.

Modern Assertiveness is a mindset and approach to life that should form the foundation on which to build *all* interactions.

True assertiveness should be as much about determining how best to communicate our opinion, as it is about recognising the moments to remain silent. Recognising how to best express and present our ideas, as well recognising the moments where the best option is to *choose* to say nothing. Not because we don't know how, or lack confidence to express our opinion effectively, but rather because we are confident that not expressing an opinion is the correct response for a specific situation.

> *Possessing the ability to choose to say nothing, is just as important as choosing the right thing to say.*

Modern Assertiveness drives interactions in which we maintain a strong sense of self-respect for our own needs and desires, but it is balanced with having respect and consideration for those we communicate with and influence. Consideration is given to the way we impact the lives of others, influence their ability to achieve their own goals, and influence their ability to maintain their own levels of self-respect.

A communication style founded on this mutually beneficial perspective is ideal as it also underpins and supports the development of a healthy balance between internal and external self-awareness. It is not about techniques and tricks to get what we want, which simply amounts to manipulation. It is about techniques and a mindset to constructively express our ideas, to constructively listen to other's ideas, and to then communicate clearly, confidently, and most importantly, respectfully.

The Skilled Communicator

The ability to effectively communicate our opinions, and the way we respond to other people's opinions, is critical to achieving success. Not only how we communicate, but how we *think* about communicating is critical. In addition, our ability to correctly read social cues and emotions is significant.

Think of it like a car. No matter the strength of the engine, the quality of the suspension, or the grip of the tyres and brakes, a significant deficiency in any of these three components will mean the car is going nowhere fast.

Here, the tyres and brakes are the communication skills of the individual – the *Communication Intelligence* (CQ). They represent the ability to effectively articulate ideas and their meaning. These are the skills that assist us to select the best words, terms, phrases and techniques to take us in our desired direction. Skills that support us to avoid inflaming situations and sending our interactions down an undesirable path to a less than satisfactory outcome.

Modern Assertiveness is a crucial ingredient of these skills.

The engine of the car is the *Intelligence* (IQ) of the individual. This represents the power to think and rationally evaluate a situation and its multiple variables and aspects.

Finally, the suspension, chassis and steering are the *Emotional Intelligence* (EQ) of the individual. This represents the ability to read social cues, monitor responses and gently guide shifts in behaviour. To listen keenly and gain a sense of the flow of our communications – how and when to push forward, and how and when to pull back.

Combined, our CQ enables the IQ and EQ to be effectively translated into productive outcomes. All components are critical to success. Equally, success cannot be achieved with an overreliance, deficiency or disregard of any specific component.

A skilled *Modern Assertiveness* communicator makes best use of their CQ, EQ and IQ skills: being acutely self-aware to identify blind spots or deficiencies in each of these key areas to engage in effective dialogue.

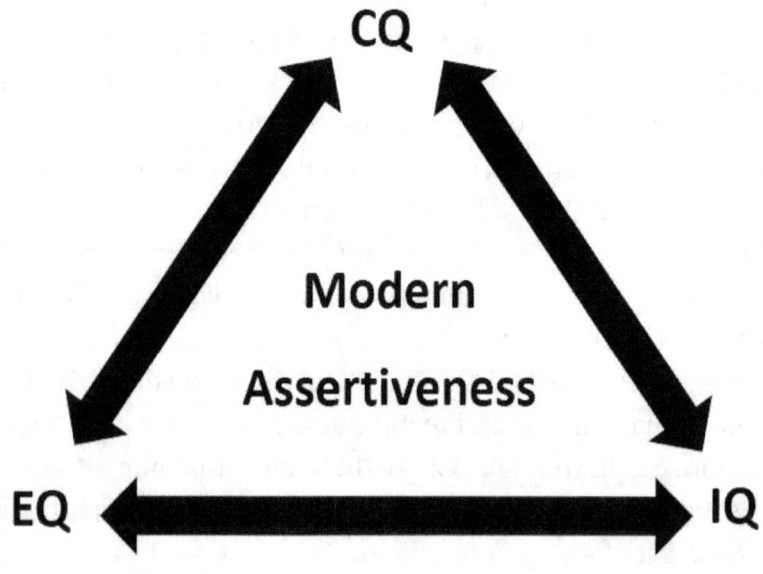

Critical Self-Analysis

To advance our communication skills, we must critically and honestly challenge all aspects of our thinking and approaches to people and situations. This analytical approach assists us to better understand what motivates and drives our behaviours. It is also needed to correctly identify and remove destructive and counter-productive motivators and drivers. We must rid ourselves of habits that have been founded on bullshit-laden advice.

Take time to reflect on the following three elements to commence a process of identifying bullshit habits and practices that need to be challenged within your current communication style.

- **Poor Motivation and Intent** – What are you *really* trying to achieve? What *really* drives you? Why are you involved, or not involved, in certain situations and communications?
- **Limiting Positions** – Why do you adopt different positions in your thinking and opinions? Is it driven by prior experiences that limit your openness or ability to respond to change? What are your fallback positions that you adopt without conscious thought? Do you take a position for comfort, or for self-protection? Do you adopt positions purely for the fun of it, to be annoying, or to be a thorn in someone's side?
- **Closed Thinking** – Do you approach situations, individuals or groups in a manner driven by bias or stereotypes? Are you truly open-minded, or do you assume closed perspectives based on assumptions? Do you engage in interactions blinkered by a predetermined position? Is your focus on finding proof

that will reinforce your initial position, irrespective of its validity and robustness?

Poor Motivation and Intent

Understanding what motivates and drives our intentions, and therefore our behaviours, is something many of us may have little interest in doing. This can be driven by several reasons: laziness, not recognising the need for change, a lack of self-awareness, or even feeling insufficiently skilled to attempt it.

But a cyclical scenario is created regardless of the underlying reason. A lack of self-awareness reinforces an inability to understand our own behaviours, which in turn, reinforces a lack of self-awareness.

The ability to remain focused on our objective is essential for engaging in positive communications. This focus underpins successful communication by enabling us to screen-in and screen-out behaviours that will either aid or hinder the realisation of our objectives.

Simply put, we need to remove impulsive responses and behaviours driven by emotional moments and the heat of the action. Again, this is where the notion of a moral compass is beneficial to guide our behaviours. Using this compass ensures we don't stray into conversational dead ends, counterproductive topics, unnecessary distractions, or negative pitfalls. It *guides* our screening process.

Far too often I have worked with organisations where directionless and objective lacking interactions are prevalent. Let me be clear. I'm not saying we must plan with precision how to navigate every single situation and interaction to gain the most beneficial outcome. That would be exhausting and exceptionally time consuming. But we do need a sense of the correct path to take. And we do need to possess the ability to spot when we are heading into dangerous territory or have taken a wrong turn.

By having a strong communication compass, we can better recognise when our comments and interactions are inflaming. When they are counterproductive, and when they are productive. Far too often conversations are driven by the wrong intentions, or poorly considered objectives.

Take providing constructive feedback as a simple example. If the objective of a conversation is to provide constructive feedback to a person on a particular topic (let's call it Topic A), then why do we so often feel the need to slip in unrelated feedback on Topics B, C, D and E while we are at it? Is it a lack of planning? Lack of time? Lack of direction? The original objective (constructive feedback on Topic A) is diluted, and the feedback compromised.

The recipient of our feedback is now overwhelmed, deflated, and de-motivated. Critically, the original objective – feedback on Topic A – is lost.

We need to understand what drives us. This understanding will help maintain a correct focus on what we are seeking to achieve. This is a critical component of effective, productive, and appropriately focused high-quality communications.

Reviewing Your Communication Compass

How could you improve your communication compass? Do you even have a communication compass?

In what interactions does it lack clear direction or send you spinning in circles?

Limiting Positions

Understanding the patterns of the various positions we adopt is crucial for developing assertive communications. Prior experiences, both successes and failures, may blinker or blind us to alternative positions and viewpoints. Prior experiences and a 'been there, done that' mentality can be useful tools to help us cope with the ever-increasing demands on our time and intellectual capability and capacity. But they are also dangerous bedfellows, as they can result in narrow-mindedness and stifle creative thinking.

There are numerous drivers of limiting positions. These include previous experience of other participants in an interaction, or of the topic at hand. They may be driven by deeply rooted opinions and perceptions. Perhaps some aren't even directly related to the topic before us, but they carry similarities that either consciously or subconsciously impact our decision-making processes. They may be conflicts encountered in childhood, or other key formative moments of our lives, that continue to resonate and influence the way we interact.

It may be a difficult process to undertake, but a critical self-review of the trends in our behaviours can lead to valuable insights that will assist us to better understand our emotional reactions to specific events. We can then look to develop specific skills and strategies to better manage and shift our responses.

There is significant value to be gained from reflecting on the interactions that make us feel uncomfortable. To consider the components of the event or interaction. To consider our emotional, physical, and psychological responses. We can then identify the emotional responses that begin to build, even at the thought of a specific event.

Some of these self-reflections and connections are easy to make. Perhaps there was an extremely aggressive manager in our past who relied heavily on intimidation and bullying.

It would be completely understandable if, years later, performance feedback discussions still made our palms sweat, our stomach twist, and raised feelings of anxiety and fear – regardless of the empathy and support demonstrated by our current manager. In this situation, the key is to put the fear into perspective, and focus on identifying tangible evidence that will reduce the fear. Evidence that demonstrates the new situation *is* different. The objective is to remove any tendencies to selectively search for, and disproportionally focus on, information that only reinforces and perpetuates fear.

Therefore, some of the positions we adopt, and emotions that seem to appear out of nowhere, can be connected to long-forgotten events. The aggressive first manager, a friendship gone wrong, or even a small offence or grievance that has festered unchecked for years to create a warped perception of a specific individual or event. It is how they continue to limit us *now* that we must recognise and address.

Reviewing Your Position

Reflect on the positions you adopt across a range of interactions. Reflect on the positions you fear, or fail, to adopt.

Then embark on a process of insightful understanding to assist identify strategies to work past fears and remove limiting positions.

Consider alternatives for each. What skills must be learnt? What mindset challenged? What entrenched behaviours shifted?

Closed Thinking

Sometimes it's advantageous to make use of our assumptions in an interaction. Drawing on prior learnings and experience can save time and allow us to get immediately to the point. We may be too time poor to wait and hear the entire story. We may lack the motivation to collect every relevant piece of information and insight before moving forward.

Particularly when workloads are high, it can be a necessary evil to move quickly, jump to conclusions, and make snap decisions. In these situations, the highly skilled and aware communicator quickly draws upon prior learnings and experiences appropriately. But they also remain observant and attentive well beyond the point of moving to a conclusion. This continuation of listening/observing/listening/observing is the key, as they continue to monitor and gauge reactions to their communications and adjust accordingly.

But prior learnings and experience can be dangerous if we merely jump from one conclusion or situation to the next, without continually questioning, monitoring and listening. Poorly used, prior learnings and experiences act to limit our perspective, narrow our view, and make us draw conclusions based on preconceived ideas in isolation. We then respond in a manner that fails to consider the outcomes. We stop listening and observing and fall into a trap of decide/deliver/decide/deliver.

To counter this trap, refinement and adjustment must be critical components of our interactions. Our prior knowledge and experience must be used to allow us to move forward and progress with speed and intelligence.

We must remain attentive and vigilant to ensure our knowledge and experience don't stifle creative thought and insightful responses.

Reviewing Your Thinking

Make note of situations where your tendency is to be closed in your thinking. What are the drivers? Is it the messenger, the topic, or perhaps the setting?

What are constructive alternatives? Are you holding onto prejudices and stereotypes that need to be called out and broken down?

Have you, without realising, extrapolated the outcomes from one bad situation to apply across many other situations? Is there a need to be better recognise that these other situations are sufficiently different or unrelated?

A Reminder – Avoid the Bullshit Feedback Sandwich

One of the best examples of a poor – yet often used – communication practice is the classic 'feedback sandwich.' I prefer to call it the 'Shit Sandwich.' It is a three-step model for giving feedback that I strongly advise against.

The idea is simple: start with positive praise, deliver the critical feedback, then finish with positive praise.

Step 1: *'Hi Mark, I know you are a great learner.'*

Step 2: *'Unfortunately, there are several mistakes in your report that need to be fixed immediately.'*

Step 3: *'But I know you are good enough to get the job done quickly.'*

At first glance this seems like a handy little technique to use. It's clear, it's concise, and it's positive. But is it? What if this approach were used all the time? Instead of being positive, the recipient of the feedback could instead interpret it as follows:

Step 1: Bread – Oh no. Am I being set up for something again (what have I done)?

Step 2: Shit – Ahh... there it is. That is the real reason for talking to me.

Step 3: Bread – What a patronising and condescending note to end on.

This is not a good communication technique. The added danger is that Steps 1 and 3 can empower the feedback provider to be excessively blunt at Step 2. The belief being that this step is so wrapped up in positivity, that it can be delivered with extreme directness. The "sandwich" can foster a lack of constructive feedback. And typically, most of us can see right through the approach.

The alternative is to focus on providing constructive and developmentally focused feedback. Feedback where the entire message is aimed at providing constructive assistance that is tailored to the individual's needs and the specific situation.

Consider instead delivering a straightforward message that sticks to the facts: 'Hi Mark, I'm concerned there are number of mistakes in the report. I need them corrected by close of business today. Is that ok? Thank you.'

The motivation is pure. The intent is clear. And the message remains genuine.

And of course, depending on the response, this approach opens up the opportunity to gain deeper understanding, work past obstacles and to educate.

Chapter 10

Loving the Sound of Your Own Voice

Speaking too Much

Speak less and listen more. This should be our ultimate communication goal.

A stronger focus on listening is a pivotal ingredient needed to assist us sift through bullshit advice to identify constructive and beneficial information, and to realise a holistic and complete self-awareness profile that is both internally and externally robust.

A greater focus on active listening supports a stronger focus on learning – acquiring knowledge and better understanding how we are perceived by and impact others.

But one of the most significant shortcomings in modern communication is a poor balance between the level of focus we give to *listening*, and the level of focus we give to *talking*. All too often the bias is excessively orientated towards talking. To communicate our position and needs with too strong a focus on self.

A quote that captures the ideal communication balance is derived from the Prayer of St Francis:

> 'Seek first to understand before seeking to be understood.'
>
> St Francis of Assisi

To support this notion, the most important sentence in our communication repertoire should not be a well-articulated comment that bamboozles, wins the argument, or shoots down a position. It shouldn't be a sentence that is full of awe-inspiring facts and figures. And it definitely shouldn't end with a full stop or an exclamation mark.

What then should it be? It should be a sentence that ends with a question mark. A sentence that has the intent to discover. A sentence designed to acquire knowledge. It is a sentence that focuses on better understanding another's experiences, emotions and needs.

> *The most important sentence ends with a question mark.*

A director at a large health organisation once told me of the high regard in which their CEO was held. A key indicator of the quality and authenticity of the CEO's style was his questioning. When all others had finished asking questions, he would ask additional and highly pertinent questions. These gleaned further information and insights. He would go deeper and understand further. Only then would he offer his opinion, proffer advice or, when needed, provide strong direction and clear instruction. The result was an extremely high level of buy-in, agreement and commitment from staff – even when the advice or message delivered was difficult.

The Lost Skill of Listening

Unfortunately, we are losing our listening skills. We are losing the ability to actively listen so that we identify the right question to ask. To ask the *right question,* at the *right time,* and in the *right way*.

Questioning effectively, to gain deeper and detailed understanding, is indeed a skill. It is a skill that needs to be mastered through constant practice, self-reflection, and personal development. The decline of this skill is a symptom of the excessive focus on developing internal self-awareness, and a neglect of external self-awareness.

There are many fundamental flaws in the way we listen. American educator and author Stephen Covey put it succinctly when he said:

> *'Most people do not listen with the intent to understand, they listen with the intent to reply.'*

Stephen Covey

The mental effort we afford to thinking of what to say next can all too frequently far outweigh the effort we afford to listening. The danger is that we are only waiting for our turn to respond. We are not actively listening to ensure we both question and respond accordingly.

To change this dynamic, we need to become skilled at questioning and responding in a manner that is free from preconceived ideas and assumptions.

To listen truly and genuinely.

The focus of an ideal approach to communication was also summarised perfectly by the Greek philosopher Epictetus:

> 'We have two ears and one mouth so that we can listen twice as much as we speak.'

Epictetus

A Lack of Questioning and Listening

If we take pause to observe our environment, it is easy to quickly both see and hear many examples of poor listening play out with disastrous and emotional outcomes. Take, for example, the response to Australia's worsening bushfire seasons. Each year, Australia's magnificent bushland burns. Whole communities are destroyed. Lives are lost. Beautiful species of flora and fauna unique to Australia teeter on the edge of extinction. And while all this plays out, politicians do what they do best: they politicise the situation and play word games.

Everyone claims that they – and they alone – have the right solution. Everyone else, they declare, is wrong. But the bullshit here that upsets me most is that there is an excessive focus on telling. Too few are asking questions and *really* listening. Listening to the scientists. Listening to the warnings from the climate and environmental experts. Listening to the indigenous custodians of the land. Listening to those that have faced the destructive ferocity of the flames and watched on as they lost everything. Those who have simultaneously felt guilt and euphoria as they watched their own house spared, but their neighbours' house obliterated.

The internet overflows with ill-considered comments and utterly flawed arguments. Fingers must be aching from being pointed, and throats hoarse from blaming.

Sadly, our response to such disasters reflects how we respond all too often in many situations. An excessive focus on telling others what to think, as opposed to listening and hearing how others feel. Giving advice, as opposed to understanding how others are impacted, so that we may correctly identify what support and solutions are needed to move forward.

An unlikely source for an excellent reminder of the powerful impact of listening before giving advice comes from American gothic rocker Marilyn Manson. Known for pushing boundaries through his confronting rock persona, and highly charged and provocative lyrics, Manson provided an extremely insightful comment when interviewed for Michael Moore's documentary *Bowling for Columbine*. Moore's documentary focused on the tragic high school shooting massacre that occurred at Columbine High School in 1999.

At the time, it was speculated Manson's violent and dark lyrics contributed to the murderous mindset of the two teenage shooters. As such, Moore asked him what he would say to the kids and community of Columbine.

Manson responded:

> *'I wouldn't say a single word to them. I would listen to what they have to say, and that's what no one did.'*

Marilyn Mason

Put aside any views and reactions you may have towards Manson's style of music and rock persona and re-read that statement: *'I would listen... and that's what no one did.'* It is an exceptionally powerful statement. It is statement from which many world leaders could learn a highly valuable lesson.

Social Media Platforms

Another piece of self-indulgent and imbalanced communication bullshit is demonstrated by a growing obsession to post content on social media platforms. Andy Warhol famously quipped that we will all have '15 minutes of fame.' Now it appears we are pursuing a thousand instances of a few *seconds* of fame.

We work to create that illusive "viral" post where huge numbers of people engage. But this is yet another example of talking, with zero listening. In fact, in too many cases it can suggest narcissism, even if unintentional. The content can be so self-indulgent and frequent that it can provide a sense of excessive self-importance – a blind spot to perceived narcissism is therefore potentially created.

Unfortunately, this is not solely the domain of socially orientated forums. It is equally prevalent on business platforms. More and more inventive ways are being found to further demonstrate a focus on telling rather than listening. The concept of listening on these platforms may seem counter intuitive, but I would personally love to see a greater percentage of posts asking for clarification and further insights. 'Hey Mark, I loved your post about removing bullshit. Can you tell me more?' It conveys a greater sense of listening, and therefore learning. Instead, the responses lean towards telling. 'Hey Mark, that's the wrong bullshit. Let me tell you what you should be doing.'

But no, for too many the key focus, the obsession, is to post and tell. And come on, let's be blunt here. So much of what is posted is pointless bullshit that adds little or no value to anyone's life.

I have seen many posts from self-proclaimed marketing gurus who declare themselves as "experts" in using social media platforms. "Experts" who will strengthen your market profile and drive quantifiable step changes in revenue growth (consultant bullshit-speak there at its best). It is emphasised that a sound social media engagement strategy should consist of daily interactions to keep audiences engaged and connected. This could be a simple 'like,' a share, a comment of agreement, or perhaps even a question to seek further information (noting the latter is used far less frequently). But astoundingly, it appears too many see this advice as a green light to post "unique personal content." Every. Single. Day.

And by "content" I don't mean something insightful, enlightening, or educational. No, frequently it's just inane and pointless *bullshit*.

Let me provide an example of something I recently read on a business orientated platform. It was a post from someone who shared that – *'they had nothing to share.'* To share to their network and the professional world at large that they had woken up that day and drawn a blank. Zip. Empty. The creativity well was dry. So, their post was about 'not having a post.' Hey presto – we now have a post. Disaster averted.

Nothing to say? Nothing to share? No inspiring little quote or story to tell? What to do? I know – post that I have no post. The default option was not to ask and acquire knowledge. It was to remain unwaveringly focused on telling. And if even if we have nothing to say? Well just say that. Given many of the posts from this individual were typically light weight dribble anyway, I was somewhat surprised that their mouth had dried up.

But what made this particular post so memorable was that someone actually had the audacity to respectfully suggest that maybe, just maybe, the better strategy when you have nothing of value to say is to... say nothing.

Well, let the hate begin.

I was left dumbfounded as this piece of valuable and empathetically delivered advice was pounced upon, abused, attacked, and demeaned. A chorus of defensive and angry responses followed 'Ignore the haters.' 'How rude.' 'They have no idea what they are talking about!'

But wait, there is a happy ending to my example. The responses whetted the original poster's appetite to feed additional senseless posts. Now there was a new fresh topic to unpack: harmony. It presented a gold mine for future posts.

They could now write about the importance of allowing the expression of opinions (the original opinion, not the empathetic advice) without hateful reactions. The need to respect the rights of other to verbalise that they have nothing to verbalise ensued. The creativity well had now been completely refilled.

The Erosion of Empathy?

What traits do we now value most? The ability to self-promote? The ability to show how much smarter we are than the next person?

But what about basic humanistic traits, such as humility, decency, and empathy? The bias toward *telling* instead of *listening*, is slowly eroding these key traits. Traits that connect us together. Traits that assist us build highly inclusive work environments and communities. It is this bias that also supports self obsession instead of self-awareness.

Again, external self-awareness is unachievable when a lack of listening inhibits our ability to comprehensively understand our impact on others. It even appears to undermine our willingness to accept constructive and well-meaning feedback!

A Reminder – Always Seek First to Understand

A while back I received a valuable reminder regarding the danger of assumptions, even when they seem both reasonable and plausible. It reminded me of the need to always understand a situation before offering an opinion or jumping to a conclusion – to effectively question and listen first.

I was standing outside my children's school, waiting to collect them at the end of the day, when I noticed a car attempting to pull into its driveway. However, the driveway was blocked by another car illegally parked across the entrance, its driver sitting inside.

I watched as the first car inched its way along a footpath between the illegally parked car and a fence. Finally, after much painstaking effort and considerable maneuvering, the car reached its destination and safely parked. To my dismay, the driver of the illegally parked car ignored the entire situation and made no attempt to move. My assumption was that the owner of the house had just struggled to park in their drive, while an illegally parked car blocked access to their own property. I was disgusted at the selfishness displayed.

Out of the now parked car came a parent with a young child in tow. As she happened to walk past me towards the school, I politely enquired if I should ask the driver of the car illegally parked across her driveway to move. I was concerned the parent was too fearful of confrontation to talk to the other driver. I was worried the same parking maneuver performed in reverse would be near impossible to complete if she needed to leave again immediately.

Her answer? 'It's ok, that's not my house. I just couldn't be bothered looking for a park, so I squeezed in there instead.'

Yes indeed: always ask questions before assuming you understand a situation. And always listen carefully before choosing your next action.

The outcome? I decided not to get involved!

Chapter 11

The Alternative - Effective Listening and Questioning

Getting the Balance Right

There are a number of key strategies that can help improve the balance between how much we love hearing the sound of our own voice, and how much we listen to the voice of others.

These strategies can develop a stronger focus on the notion of 'seeking first to understand before being understood.' They are strategies that lead to genuine interactions, and deeper and longer lasting relationships. They are also strategies that will assist in the development of a robust and complete self-awareness profile.

Empathy

The first key strategy is empathy. A basic premise of empathy is to focus on understanding the emotions, experiences, and opinions of others.

Unfortunately, empathy is commonly defined as putting ourselves in someone else's shoes. But in fact, that is not the concept at all. A key shift for this analogy to be correct is in the perspective. Empathy is not about understanding our own perspective, but about understanding the perspective of others. This is the crucial element. Empathy, therefore, is correctly defined as understanding how someone else feels in their *own* shoes.

The danger of the first definition is that it can drive assumptions and preconceived ideas. Worse still, it can be driven by subconscious thinking. Thinking where we inadvertently project on to others what we consider to be their thoughts and opinions, but based on how we would react to a similar situation. In effect, this definition drives behaviour in complete opposition to the true notion of empathy.

Consider this. Years ago, a client relayed a conversation she had had with a close friend who had just lost her family home in a natural disaster. Wanting to be empathetic and supportive, she had called to tell the friend that 'she knew how she felt.' My client lamented that as soon the statement came from her mouth, she could hear precisely how wrong it was. It was both presumptive and it was clumsy. She herself had never experienced such a disastrous scenario. How could she possibly know how her friend felt?

Of course, the question she had really wanted to ask to convey empathy and support was a simple: 'How do you feel?' A simple empathetic question, rather than an assumptive statement.

Reviewing Your Assumptions

Reflect on the important conversations you have had in the last few days, weeks or months. Reflect on your approach. What was your style in these conversations? Were you too quick to offer advice? Did you redirect conversations into a discussion of your own experiences?

Or instead, did you focus on empathising in order to deeply understand the other person's position, thinking and feelings?

Did you ask open questions, while actively and attentively listening to the responses with a clear and open mind, free of preconceived ideas and assumptions?

Make note of any assumptions you do tend to make about the actions, inactions, and attitudes of others. Are these assumptions based on fact or fiction?

Are they assumptions based on a single observed instance of behaviour, or multiple instances?

Ask Another Question

Through my work, I encounter a broad range of staff behavioural problems that leaders must effectively manage. Supporting team members who have lost motivation, turning around poor performance, removing dysfunctional or toxic behaviours, leading through complex and disruptive periods of change, and so on.

When I ask for detail about the specifics of a situation, far too frequently there are significant and glaring gaps in the information I am subsequently provided. How can I possibly provide effective advice, or suggest a suitable solution, if the leader doesn't even possess a detailed understanding of what is before them? Just as significantly, how can the leader possibly solve the problem with any great effect unless they also know more?

These knowledge gaps are typically populated, or perhaps a better word would be polluted, with assumptions. Therefore, the resulting solutions and strategies that are founded on assumptions are often flawed, and frequently fail.

A significant perspective to challenge is the frequency with which our mindset is incorrectly driven by assumptions, or correctly driven by relevant acquired knowledge of a given situation.

As a result, a significant portion of my work is spent supporting skill development to enable the effective acquisition of relevant knowledge and insights. To correctly fill knowledge gaps in order to make, and execute, well thought-out plans.

But how exactly is this achieved?

In part, we must learn to ask a question, then another, and when we think we have asked enough, think about whether we still need to ask another and another.

Some useful self-reflective questions to challenge effective knowledge gathering include:

- Do I have all the information I need to make a sound decision or give sound advice?
- Are there any blind spots or gaps in my knowledge and my view of this situation?
- Have I removed all pre-conceived ideas?
- Have I empowered everyone involved to offer their frank and honest opinion?

That last question can be a difficult one to answer. It requires a critical self-analysis of our personal leadership and communication style.

Don't worry, I'll cover how to do that in Chapter 16. And of course, identify some leadership bullshit along the way!

Shifting a Current Conversation

Consider a difficult scenario you currently face.

Do you fully understand the situation and the position/views/opinions of all involved? What additional questions should you be asking?

What types of questions do *you* need to make sure you include in your repertoire?

Conflict Maps

A helpful way to breakdown complex scenarios and interactions is to use a Conflict Map.

Conflict Maps provide a structured methodology to consider all potential issues and obstacles when preparing for difficult dialogues. They are also exceptionally powerful at driving highly informative discussions.

A Conflict Map template is provided below.

Of course, the map can be adjusted to include as many participants as necessary. Start by outlining the scenario, then identify and map out the key drivers, obstacles, participants, and concerns.

Finally, consider what knowledge gaps exist, and therefore, what critical questions still need to be asked. Trust me, using this structured and planned approach works.

What is the scenario?	
How did it start? What are the drivers?	
What are key obstacles to overcome?	
Who are the participants?	
Person 1	Person 2
Needs?	Needs?
Concerns?	Concerns?
Impact?	Impact?
Opportunities?	Opportunities?

Conflict Map

Listening Pitfalls

Shifting our focus to an empathetic position greatly improves our listening. However, there are numerous pitfalls that we must avoid falling into.

Below are three of the pitfalls great listeners effectively manage to avoid.

1. Biased listening

Listening with bias, and preconceived ideas, is something we must actively work to remove.

We must remain vigilant and not allow what we expect to hear to unduly influence and restrict the effectiveness of our listening. We must work to ensure we hear what is *actually* being said; not what we *think* is being said.

If not managed well, our experiences and prior knowledge become a proverbial ball and chain attached to our ankle: holding us back by stifling our ability to effectively see and hear alternatives. We must strive to hear a message without bias, as opposed to determining the value of the message based on the perceived merit or likeability of the messenger, or other irrelevant or unrelated factors.

We must all strive to be sufficiently self-confident so that we are able to keep our ears and eyes wide open to *hear* what is actually being said. To suspend our internal dialogue, and not be thinking of what to say next. To focus on hearing accurately, to process information correctly, and then – and only then – provide a relevant and connected response by correctly tapping into our expansive knowledge bank.

Even further, we must be comfortable not always having an immediate answer, and not feeling foolish should we need to ask additional questions and need more time to respond. These are critical steps in the learning journey as we shift from novice to true expert.

The highly skilled listener's focus is well aligned to, and supports, the 'seek first to understand before being understood' mindset.

2. Information overload

The second pitfall is information overload. The amount of stimulus that we are bombarded with day in and day out can be overwhelming.

Consider the moment you are in right now as you read these words. You are processing the letters and words on the page. Perhaps there is the physical sensation of your seat? Perhaps there are external sounds around you? Traffic, chatter of people, or perhaps the neighbour's dog who always seems to know exactly when to start barking for maximum irritation?

Now consider conversations with one person. Consider conversations with multiple people. Again, there are numerous background distractions and stimuli that our brain must take in and process. With all these competing and distracting stimuli, we must still accurately hear what is being said *and* process this information quickly and logically.

Hopefully by now, you are starting to think about how to remove habits such as biased listening. But what of processing new and complex information? Correctly assimilating information with knowledge already possessed, and all while an ongoing conversation occurs.

To cope with the level of information we must process, our brain adopts short-cuts. We chunk information together so that we can quickly process, and better remember, large amounts of information. We then use our prior experience and learnings to identify known and perceived patterns in order to reduce the burden of determining our response strategies.

But when rapidly inundated with large amounts of information, these short-cuts can result in the illogical chunking together of information. The consequence can be the drawing of illogical inferences, conclusions, and therefore opinions and proffered responses.

I demonstrate this in workshops using a simple, but effective, activity. First, I inform participants that I will describe a scenario and then ask a question at the end. I then proceed to describe a scenario in excessive detail. Long-winded, verbose statements overloaded with small snippets of information. Numbers, colours, locations, names – *anything* to add an excessive amount of information to be process within a tight time constraint. At the end of my drawn-out and detailed description, I ask a related, but completely nonsensical, question.

When asked on its own, it is a question that would draw a response of confusion. On its own, participants would point out the sheer stupidity of the question. But when asked immediately following the detailed description, participants are so distracted and focused on the content of the story just heard, that they attempt to answer my illogical question with a logical response.

It is amusing to hear, but it memorably illustrates my point to the participants – beware of information overload.

Painting a detailed scenario in this way, and then asking a nonsensical question, renders the participants passive in the interaction. They have assumed a role focused purely on listening intently. Prior learnings and chunking of information kicks in as they attempt to retain all the facts. Information is pieced together, and conclusions are drawn in a manner that their logic and experiences dictate.

But all this processing causes a fatal assumption to be made – that my question *will* be logical. With that taken as a given, the question is not afforded sufficient focus. Consequently, the question is misheard so that it logically fits with the scenario. In this instance, information overload causes biased listening. Participants hear what they expect to be said, not what is actually said.

Of course, a simple way to manage these processing shortcomings is to ensure we not only actively listen, but actively *participate* in conversations. How? Politely interjecting with questions to clarify information that lacks detail. Paraphrase and summarise content heard to verify we are on the right track and processing information correctly. And, most importantly, give ourselves the time needed to process information accurately, and respond accordingly.

To support taking the time needed to respond correctly, we must also appreciate moments of silence. These moments allow us that extra second or three to mull things over in our mind. To ask ourselves a number of inquisitive, fact-checking and processing questions before responding.

But we must keep in mind that we don't always have to respond immediately. Great communicators are comfortable to defer and delay a response until a later point in time. They don't allow themselves to be pushed to respond poorly in the moment when overwhelmed or unsure.

Great communicators respond as best as possible when the time is right. This is not about avoiding a conversation or avoiding a response. It is about controlling the dialogue. It is about delaying a response until we are ready to best proceed.

However, there are two important tips to keep in mind:

- **Don't be a parrot** – paraphrasing is a great way to assist in the correct processing of information, but don't overdo it. Too many take this approach and put it on steroids. The result is a parrot who repeats back almost every word they hear, to a point where it becomes exceptionally distracting and irritating.
- **Don't delay to avoid** – if you defer all interactions and difficult conversations to a later point in time, it can be a sure sign that your claimed strategy of delaying has become a thinly veiled excuse to avoid. Particularly if you delay using a vague and undefined time frame. 'Later' is not a firm time commitment.

3. Being in the moment

Not being in the moment is another of the modern-day afflictions that negatively impacts the effectiveness of our communications. What I'm referring to is a lack of being 100% mentally present in our interactions. Being fully in each moment – effectively blocking out all the noise, the distractions, and competing demands for our attention. Being focused on the conversation at hand that requires our conscious input. Being able to put down the last moment we were mentally engaged in. Being fully prepared for the next moment the instant it begins. And always, being able to quickly spot when our focus fades or deviates away from the current moment, so that we may avoid the 'lights are on, but no one is home' style of interaction.

I view this issue as a modern-day affliction, as our lives are now drowning in competing demands. More than ever, we are attempting to juggle an absurd number of balls at once.

And now, on top of this, we have introduced two additional factors:

- **Ridiculous amounts of stress-inducing expectation** and pressure to do more and more
- **Extreme levels of connectivity** through technology which results in us always being plugged in. We are constantly looking at our smart phones to read emails, check the weather, or see what a friend is up to.

We must STOP! We must regain control of our focus. We need to be *in* the moment. We need to better provide our complete and undivided attention to demonstrate that nothing else matters beyond the interaction we are currently in.

Achieving this can be hard. But the reward of having genuine and focused conversations will repay you enormously, for these types of conversations underpin the development of empathy, trust, and authenticity. As such, we are more likely to gain buy-in from others to our ideas, strategies, and opinions.

Above all else, we actively hear all of the information – not just bits and pieces picked up between checking our phone ten times, thinking about what happened in a previous conversation, or what will happen in the next.

Level of Presence

There are simple actions you can take to immediately improve your level of presence, and achieve lasting change with persistence and practice:

1. Manage your phone. First step: turn off notifications for all Apps that don't need to be instantly read. Few, if any, need your constant and immediate attention. It is ridiculous the number of times I have observed people mid-conversation distracted by their phone lighting up with an unimportant notification.
Second step: turn it off completely when having important conversations. If this isn't possible, at a minimum turn it screen down so as not to be distracted (I'll assume it has already been put on silent).

2. Clear your mind. Before approaching your next interaction, work to clear your mind. Clear it of irrelevant thoughts and distractions and start to fill it with content relevant to the next interaction.
This can be done while walking from one interaction to the next, or by taking a few seconds to pause and focus before starting your next conversation. This can also be a great way of giving your mind a break between interactions.

3. Practice mindfulness. This involves paying attention to the present moment to be acutely aware of how you are responding and feeling. This self-monitoring is difficult to master and takes effort. But it is a powerful tool to assist in quickly identifying when the mind wanders.

You must become skilled at both catching when your mind wanders, and skilled at bringing yourself back to the present moment. The methods for practicing mindfulness, and achieving a mindful state, can significantly enhance your listening skills: achieving an improved focus on the present, with fewer and shorter deviations onto paths of distraction.

Improving Presence

For each of these three areas, take time to identify poor practices or habits that need adjustment.

What changes can be made to support the development of a highly present and engaged communication style?

Technology Enabled Inattention

I was driving recently when a pedestrian stepped out in front of me. Why? They were so engrossed in their phone that they were completely oblivious to their surrounds.

For all the advantages our smart devices provide us, they absorb so much of our attention that we are becoming skilled at missing significant cues that tell us our focus is needed elsewhere. Even significant cues that will prevent us from stepping out in front of an oncoming vehicle!

Our smart devices present us with a double-edged sword. While they offer greater connectivity and greater access to information, they suck away our time and focus. They now render us so oblivious to our surrounds that we can fail to adequately engage with others. A flow on effect is poor listening and questioning habits.

I see similar scenarios to my pedestrian experience play out in meetings and interactions on a daily basis. Individuals attempting to manage their focus in meetings and conversations, all while attending to emails on their phone. Checking if the notification that just popped up was about an important project, sealing a deal, or a 'hey look what I'm about to eat' plate shot from a friend.

Close your laptop in your next meeting. Put away your phone in your next conversation. Fully engage in the moment. Otherwise, before you know it, you too could be blindly stepping out in front of a car.

Taking Constructive Ownership of Our Message

Finally, when communications don't go to plan, when instructions aren't followed as required, or when we dislike feedback received, it is extremely easy to deflect, finger point, or blame others. But it is important to avoid a negative mindset in these situations. 'They didn't listen properly.' 'They weren't paying attention.' 'They're just being lazy.' These are all mindsets that must be avoided.

In fact, it is these mindsets that are lazy. They don't take constructive ownership of how to best convey future messages. They don't support effective questioning and listening to carefully ascertain whether our communications were clear, or our messages understood.

Adopting a communication position that defaults to finger pointing and placing blame on others, particularly on their perceived failings, is extremely counterproductive. If we are not careful, we can end up adopting a negative default position that focuses on assigning blame, rather than listening, learning and adapting.

Instead, we must shift to a positive default position. One where our focus is firmly fixated on constructively evaluating how we can improve our messages. This must include an emphasis on asking self-reflective questions that are focused on achieving a deeper and more complete understanding of our communications practices, and inquisitive questions to gain comprehensive detail.

Our focus must also include a willingness to hear and take on board constructive feedback to better understand any changes required. The result will be an adaptive and responsive communication style. A style that is better able to effectively influence the range of scenarios we face, by remaining highly engaged and attentive.

Mindsets such as 'They don't trust me, what's their issue?' must shift to 'Why don't they think I have acted in a manner that demonstrates my trustworthiness?' This is followed by detailed self-reflection to identify how subsequent communications can be adjusted and improved to authentically build trust, to question effectively, and subsequently listen with an open mind.

It brings us full circle back to St Francis of Assisi:

> *'Seek first to understand before seeking to be understood.'*
>
> St Francis of Assisi

Improving Your Listening Skills

Consider whether you have any poor listening habits in need of change. Note any new strategies needed to improve listening outcomes.

Perhaps, it is being in the moment from the first word of every interaction so that you can better remember names? That is most definitely one of mine!

Perhaps it is ensuring your default listening position is firmly focused on adapting and learning, as opposed to listening to apportion blame?

A Reminder – Sometimes Saying Less is Better

I can't help myself. I'm a crowd watcher.

When I'm at large public gatherings, I note the actions and behaviours of others. Those who are helpful and courteous. Those that push through doorways. Those that open doors. Those that are oblivious to their surrounds. Those that are not.

One year, while spectating at the Australian Open Tennis, I observed an intriguing outcome. It was a men's second-round match. One of the top seeds was playing a rank outsider. The seeded player had several highly passionate and vocal clusters of supporters scattered throughout the stands.

I love listening to passionate supporters. Their chants and yells of support add an extra level of atmosphere and enjoyment to the game. But in this match, one exceptionally passionate supporter went too far.

What started as a crowd of 5,000 fans predominantly supporting the seeded player, quickly turned into the vast majority shouting support for the underdog. But how could this happen?

One lone, passionate supporter turned the atmosphere in the stadium by failing to pick up on cues of when to stop screaming her support over the top of others. It was exceptionally loud and emotional support for the seeded player, whom she hoped to marry – as was declared on her country's flag. A large flag that she incessantly waved high in the air, frequently blocking the view for several rows of spectators behind her.

If anyone yelled a word of encouragement to the underdog, she would immediately scream over the top to drown them out and supporter her player. This happened time and time again. In effect, it became a form of bullying. The rest of the crowd didn't take kindly to it.

It soon became apparent that if the crowd felt she was yelling over them, then the crowd would yell over her. Simply out of annoyance – and to drown her out. Now, when she encouraged her player, numerous yells of support for the underdog would immediately follow.

The game turned into a long and hard fought five-set match that went for hours. The crowd cheering ecstatically for each point the underdog won. Screams of emphatic support for each game claimed as he increasingly looked exhausted and near collapse. And the result? After much struggle, and coming perilously close to defeat, the underdog claimed the win to the thunderous applause of the crowd.

In his on-court post-game interview, the victor acknowledged the crowd's support. 'I would like to thank the crowd; I was feeling exhausted toward the end, and your fantastic support helped pick me up and get me over the line. I don't think I could have won without you.'

The lesson to be learnt by that lone passionate supporter? Always respect the opinions of others – even when they are counter to our own. Yelling louder and yelling last does not make your opinion better. And it won't necessarily give you what you hoped for.

In fact, it may give you the complete opposite!

Chapter 12

Annoying "Inspirational" Statements

What are They Really?

How many times have you heard them?

Those often-touted golden gems of supposed inspiration. Those wonderful little lines often quoted by the latest self-help guru or life coach.

How many times have you seen them? On your LinkedIn feed, your Facebook feed, print media, online media. Everywhere. Those insidious – and frequently pointless – "inspirational" statements.

The same quote is often attributed to various sources – business leaders, politicians, sports people. Anyone who appears to give the comment greater authenticity and bite for the person sharing it. The old 'fake it until you make it' type of comment. What does that even mean? What does it inspire? Lie and deceive until you work out how something should be done?

The examples are numerous. 'You can be whatever you want to be.' 'If you imagine it, it will come true.' 'If you aim high enough, you will soar.' 'If you want to be successful, you need only to stay focused.' But they are all too frequently bullshit comments that only paint half the picture.

They are comments that motivate the reader to embark on potentially pointless and stress-inducing pursuits of irrational, unrealistic or ill-considered goals. And further, more frequently than not, they are aligned with pushing a self-serving focus – a pursuit of personal success without consideration of anything but our own aspirations.

Ironically, it was some of these ridiculous bullshit statements that helped motivate the birth of this book.

> *'If you aren't aiming for the stars, you aren't aiming high enough.'*

It didn't motivate me because I wanted to aim higher. Instead, it motivated me because I find it exceptionally annoying. What is it trying to inspire? Where are we supposed to be aiming? What is the context? Does the person sharing it really know me well enough to tell me that I am, or am not, aiming high enough? It smacks of a selfish, self-absorbed, and self-obsessed pursuit of more. A call to arms for selfishness. A toxic, activating ingredient for stress, anxiety, and depression. In short, it's just plain dumb.

But it doesn't end there. There are so many other variations along the lines of 'If you can dream it, imagine it, or think it, then you can be it, have it, or realise it.' Another example:

> *'If your dreams don't scare you, then they're not big enough.'*

What is this attempting to inspire? What is it hoping to promote? Personally, the word I use to refer to dreams that scare me is – nightmare! Our dreams should excite and inspire, not petrify.

But again, the focus of this statement is on more. Make it bigger, make it more. And when you've done that, make it bigger again.

Twisting Quotes and Statements

Disingenuous quotes and statements of "inspirational" advice have driven many to alter their direction in life and re-assess and shift their goals – but not for the better. Even the way we approach our dreams has changed. Where once we *chased* our dreams, now we *pursue* our dreams. The language and mindset have shifted to a more singularly focused, aggressive and self-serving tone.

Statements of supposed inspiration are bantered around and indiscriminately espoused by an exploding number of life coaches and self-help "experts." But how much damage do they cause? How many unrealistic and unachievable goals have they created for people to pursue? How many people have crashed and burned, labouring tirelessly to achieve what they drive?

I'm certain they inspire some. I'm certain some have reached a higher achievement having read them.

But I'm also certain there is a significant cost of collateral damage. Being inspired to tirelessly pursue an objective in one area of life, will almost certainly have a detrimental impact on other areas of life: relationships, personal health, perhaps our communities, or even our environment.

Surely there are better and less destructive options than these snippets of poor advice?

I have read quotes that made complete sense if used in the manner intended by their author. Statements that were aimed at a specific audience, but now thrown around indiscriminately.

Quotes that were connected to a specific *moment in time*, but now used *all the time*. And there are the quotes that have had their moment in the sun, but that sun has now set, and their ongoing use a festering cliché.

I wonder how many of those who wrote and uttered now famous words wish that they could take them back, or at least ban, or control, their use?

Realism Doesn't Sell

Unfortunately, realistic alternatives don't sell as well. I get that the following is not as "sexy" or "catchy," but it is balanced:

> *If you can imagine it, have done a comprehensive assessment of the perceivable risks, obstacles, and the most likely outcomes and benefits, coupled with a realistic timeframe and scope of requirements with a consideration of the probability of success, allowing for demand and need, and you still think it has a possibility of success…*
> *then go for it.*

The above statement is sensible and realistic. But unfortunately, the bullshit is more appealing.

Bullshit only touts the success stories: people who were inspired and "made it" – whatever or wherever "it" is. But those that are burnt out and left feeling disillusioned are conveniently ignored and forgotten by the wayside.

"Bullshit inspirers" push us to move forward with our eyes wide shut, while we tilt or head up to the stars not watching, or paying attention to, where we walk.

Imagine if an organisation were to commence a merger or acquisition with this mindset. Just imagine the successful new business we want and, hey presto, there it is. No. An organisation does its due diligence. It researches the market. It assesses and identifies obstacles that will need to be overcome. Then, and only then, will it move forward. Not always with success, but at least with eyes wide open.

The organisation is watching precisely where it walks. Every step carefully planned and then executed. There is no daydreaming about the stars.

Personal Due Diligence

It is this same level of due diligence that we as individuals often neglect to perform. We must aim to manage the steps we take in our careers, and the changes we make in our lives, with the same level of analysis, planning and execution as that used by organisations. This approach will allow us to best achieve a balance between our passions and our common sense.

When I quit my job and went out on my own back in 2007, I *was* inspired by my emotions, and I *was* inspired by some of the 'just do it' type of quotes. But that was only a very small part of my mindset.

Before I made such a massive life decision, I researched. I spoke to old clients. I spoke to prospective clients. I asked them if they would work with me as *me*. Not me as part of a large consulting company with their mass of intellectual knowledge and know-how behind me.

Only when I had enough yes responses, and I had a clear idea of what my business model would encompass, then – and only then – did I step forward.

I *wasn't* thinking about the stars. I *was* thinking about viability. I was thinking about what would be around the next corner, and the next and the next.

The outcome? Many years on and I couldn't be happier with my career shift.

I have survived a global financial crisis. I have had the opportunity to work with an amazing range of organisations, and work with many inspirational people.

But this was achieved with appropriate due diligence, planning and persistence. Not because of a meaningless quote of inspiration that drove false expectations and my head to be in the clouds.

I do absolutely believe we should aspire to be the best possible versions of ourselves and have dreams that inspire and excite us. Much of my work is focused on supporting and enabling people to realise their full potential. But we must aim for a future that will bring a balance between happiness, fulfilment, and a personal sense of accomplishment.

For this to be possible, it must be something we have personally defined that is relevant, achievable and that will provide a rewarding journey of growth. Not a journey of stress as we are pushed to chase nightmares!

Striving for a ridiculous level of success that is pushed on us by someone else's rhetoric of "more" is neither healthy, nor perhaps, even achievable. We need to set realistic goals.

We need goals that will extend us to realise our best, but goals that are founded on information and ideas that are insightful and inspiring, while tempered with realism, practicality and common sense.

The Creation of Unattainable Goals

One of the most widely used frameworks for goals setting is the SMART goals framework.

This acronym stands for:

S – Specific: focused on a clearly defined and precise area

M – Measurable: a consideration of how progress can be assessed

A – Achievable: to challenge and inspire while remaining possible

R – Relevant: to the individual and to their broader context

T – Time-bound: specifics about when the desired outcome is to be achieved

However, many "inspirational" quotes are far from aligned to this framework. In fact, they are frequently counterproductive and oppositional to all constructive frameworks for effective goal setting. Providing motivation to aim for the stars, and then in the next sentence promoting the use of SMART goals, is clearly a contradiction. But it is a contradiction I have seen many "experts" promote. Can many of the statements of inspiration truly underpin the formulation of SMART goals? Typically, they can't.

The biggest flaw is in the 'A' of the SMART goal. Are they *Achievable*? If we aim so high that we lack the fundamental resources, skills or knowledge needed to get there – then no, they are not.

Too often I have had to support individuals reinvigorate their levels of motivation, and repair their self-esteem, after being encouraged to 'aim high and dream it.' After much effort, stress and frustration, the realisation had hit home that what was aimed for was beyond them. It was out of their reach. It wasn't personally relevant. For some a fundamental ingredient for success was missing. An ingredient that could not be created or purchased. A showstopper.

Nothing is as demotivating as setting goals that can't be achieved. We never feel the joy of successful goal completion. We are instead stuck in the grind of never quite making it: a place that can be soul destroying, and exceptionally demotivating. To ensure our goals are indeed SMART, we need to be both savvy and realistic in how we create them. We must ensure we don't let our minds be filled with distracting and misleading information when formulating them.

'Toxic Positivity'

Another danger inherent in a fixation on ill-considered inspirational quotes can be the tendency to focus solely on promoting an upbeat and 'you can do this' positive mindset. While a positive mindset can be critical in the face of adversity, the lack of a balanced perspective is not.

Toxic Positivity is produced when negative emotions are regarded as bad and to be avoided. It is when there is an excessive attempt to apply positive thoughts across every circumstance encountered in life – be it good, bad or ugly. Positive platitudes become the mantra. 'It's not that bad.' 'It could be worse.' 'Don't worry, it'll be fine.'

Toxic Positivity involves excessive attempts to ignore negative situations, and the emotions they elicit. The driving focus is to remain positive and optimistic. But this strategy is not constructive to achieving a healthy state of mind. In fact, it can be significantly detrimental.

It creates a lack of self-compassion. It shuns the need to accept, process and understand negative emotions, and our reactions to these emotions. Instead, this dysfunctional mindset excessively concentrates on being happy and positive. It morphs negative emotions into something to be ashamed of, or even feel guilty, experiencing. They are perceived weaknesses to remove from our emotional and intellectual repertoire.

Cliché inspirational comments suit perfectly to this scenario. Comments that overly focus on producing positive vibes at the expense of realistic self-assessments, acceptance of negatives, and a healthy self-evaluation. The mantra of 'aim for the stars,' combined with 'just be happy,' or 'things aren't that bad; it could be worse' are a dangerous mix. They discount and discredit the insights that can be had from our negative experiences and reactions.

If we are not careful, these statements help create a mindset that includes poor self-reflection and an unwillingness to admit to, or accept, our mistakes. Grief and negativity caused by failure or loss are viewed as weaknesses to rid from our mind, as opposed to being accepted and embraced as part of the full range of human emotions from which to learn and develop.

Toxic Positivity drives a poorly balanced perspective. It focuses on only embracing one end of the full range of human emotions. It is not healthy. We must be skilled at appreciating and responding to the full range of human emotions. This must include the ability to embrace and learn from those emotions that are negative.

Further, *Toxic Positivity* helps to create unrealistic goals and expectations founded on an overly optimistic approach. The outcome?

The pursuit of hopelessly unrealistic goals with a forced or fake smile.

Chapter 13

The Alternative - Defining Statements

A Healthy Dose of Realism

Overall, the self-help and coaching industry that serves up the "inspirational" quote is helping far fewer people attain happiness and success, than it is fostering increased levels of frustration, anxiety, and stress.

The proof is in the pudding. Levels of anxiety, depression and suicide are at their highest recorded levels and the trajectory is up.

It's time for this bullshit to stop. To avoid creating unrealistic expectations and aspirations, there must also be a healthy dose of realism. Yes, aim high, work hard, and strive to be the best version of yourself. But be realistic and sensible about the road you are inspired to travel.

Take for example the number of people who aspire to be a CEO, their dreams fuelled by the 'aim for the stars' notion – they set their sights on the role that signifies the highest and brightest star. But for far too many, this aspiration appears to be accompanied by a complete lack of awareness of the commitment and sacrifice required. The hours spent at work, and the impact on non-work aspects of life. The demanding pressures, expectations and stress that will accompany the role.

Instead, the role of a CEO is placed on a pedestal, with no context or clarity of what it takes to get there. No understanding of the skills and attributes needed to succeed. But it's ok: 'I have dreamt it – so it will be *easy*.' And therefore, it will happen.

Too few give due consideration to the simple fact that the number of CEO seats are limited. A company has one CEO, but how many are aspiring to be the next? For those that don't make it to the CEO's seat, will they happily take a seat at a lower level? Will they view this as a position of failure from which to throw stones, cynical they had "their" seat stolen by another less deserving? Alternatively, will they accept that someone else better suited was appointed, and therefore provide their full and unwavering support?

Many years ago, I eavesdropped in on a conversation between two fellow passengers on my early morning train commute to work. The content of the conversation made it apparent that both were new starters as graduates at a bank. They were young and enthusiastic, fresh from university, and ready to conquer the corporate world. What caught my attention was when one made the lofty declaration that they would be a senior manager within a couple of years, and then director by the time they turned 30. To which the other agreed emphatically that they too held similar expectations. Not aspirations – expectations!

Very lofty expectations indeed. Realistic? I doubt it. But who am I to say? Perhaps they were. I knew nothing of their skills and potential, nor of the opportunities or structure of their new employer. But my concern – I wondered if they had any idea either? And I wondered, if these initial expectations weren't met, would they be capable of setting new goals and aspirations to personally challenge and motivate their continuing careers? Or would they be burnt out, disillusioned and demotivated when their 30th birthday arrived, and a director role was not theirs to be had?

Adopting a Balanced No Bullshit Goal Setting Perspective

Another bullshit aspect of many "inspirational" statements is that they are too often nonsensical. They cause disillusionment and frustration due to their potential to create self-perceptions of inadequacy and failure through unrealistic and excessive goal setting. To further add to the bullshit, they drive self-absorbed and self-interested goals, and therefore behaviours, that are too frequently *get more, have more* and *be more* orientated. Again, see the trend – another force that drives us forward at the expense of ourselves and others.

There are several highly pertinent perspectives to consider when deciding what stars to aim for. They are not perspectives to be used as an excuse to give up or not bother. They are perspectives to help make sure we are pointing ourselves in a constructive direction, and not a destructive one. A direction that can dynamically evolve and be refined as our skills and abilities shift. A direction that is within our scope to achieve through an appropriate amount of diligent hard work, commitment and, sometimes perhaps, an ounce or two of luck.

The following two questions are a great starting point to ensure the goals we set are productive and inspiring, as opposed to counterproductive and demotivating. To ensure we create goals that will not only challenge and extend us to achieve, but to also ensure they *are* in fact achievable.

These questions are not asked to justify not bothering or not trying. They are questions to understand the need, the opportunity, and then to precisely understand the level of effort, determination, and focus that will be required. It is to step forward with a plan, with a goal and with clarity of purpose – with our eyes and ears wide open!

1. *Do you possess the core traits needed to achieve your goal?*

Just because someone wants to be an astronaut, and can clearly imagine themselves doing a spacewalk, doesn't mean it will come true. Do they possess the intellectual capability required to become a world leading scientist in a profession that will be considered valuable for space exploration and research?

Does the person dreaming of being a mountain climber unknowingly suffer from vertigo? Does the person aiming to sail the seven seas unknowingly suffer from severe sea sickness?

A crucial step before setting a goal is understanding what will be required to get there, and as best as possible determining whether we possess, or lack, core traits that will prevent us from achieving success. It is part of the due diligence process. It is the realistic self-assessment component.

To not do this first raises a significant risk that we will waste much time and effort. We will experience frustration and disillusionment as our goal will never be within our reach – no matter how hard we try.

Take myself as an example. As a teenager I dreamt of playing volleyball at the Olympics. But there were two issues: my skill level and my height. The first I could train hard at to improve. Although still not realistic (I wasn't really that good at volleyball), it was still within my power to influence. The other I could not change.

I wanted to play in a sport, and in a position on the court, that would typically be filled by someone *at least* 30cms taller, and with a huge standing vertical jump.

I was simply not tall enough, nor athletic enough.

If someone had told me to chase my dreams, as I could be whatever I wanted, what would have been the result? I can guarantee you it would not have been me reaching the Olympics!

Sure, there is the exception to the rule. But for every single exception, how many thousands – or millions – of non-exceptions are there? We must have a clear understanding of what is needed to achieve success. The hours required, the money needed, the study, practice, commitment, and even the intellectual capability and physical attributes.

We must also have an appreciation of what it would take to be the exception to the rule to overcome any significant hurdles encountered. It is great to have dreams and aspirations, but we must be realistic.

We don't all have the same levels of drive and motivation to succeed. We don't all have the same levels of focus and determination to put in the hours required. Elite sports people are not successful because of physical attributes alone. They are successful because they also have the mental and physical stamina to put in longer hours, and train harder than their competitors.

2. Is there a need for it?

Not everyone can be an inventor of a flash new gadget that makes billions, a social media influencer with a million followers, or the next sports super star.

There simply are not enough spaces, places or opportunities to do so. But how many young children are now dreaming that they will be the next?

It is great to aspire and look up to something, and to work hard to achieve a dream. But how many are being told that they *will* be it. That if we can simply dream it, then it *will* come true. The number of children and, for that matter adults, who are being fed misleading information that they *will* be whatever they want scares me. This is where the first toxic seeds of unrealistic goal setting and future failures are planted. We must consider how many opportunities really exist? Will they still exist in 10 years? How competitive is it to achieve?

Reassessing Your Goals

Reflect on your current goals and aspirations.

Consider the four questions above and the SMART goals framework. Consider whether your current goals are *Achievable* and *Relevant*?

Have you undertaken a sufficient process of due diligence and review to ensure your current goals and aspirations are appropriate?

Will they motivate and inspire you to achieve success, aligned with who you *aspire to be*? Alternatively, will they drive you to a state of frustration and exhaustion as you chase dreams that are simply not for you? Dreams pushed onto you by others.

Your Defining Statements

I'm not suggesting everything we read is false. But it can be hard to resist following the latest fad, the next trend, or be cornered by the weight of expectation to get with the program and do what everyone else is doing.

Just because the masses adopt something doesn't make it right. But it may just mean a greater number will need to make a future reassessment, should they realise they have gone down the wrong path. We may like to think we are highly innovative and independent, but are we? Or are we blindly following the direction of others more than ever before?

The pursuit of erroneous and misguided "inspirational" statements has resulted in many of the negatives we must now work to remove from our workplaces: inequality, discrimination, bullying, poor leadership, and inflated egos. Further, broader feelings of personal unhappiness, dissatisfaction, and failure in life must also be removed for many.

We need to throw away the "inspirational" statement and adopt what I refer to as *Defining Statements*.

Statements that define and drive what we wish to be known for – what we wish to stand for. The positive difference that we will make to our life and the lives of others. The way we will work to lead a satisfying and less stressful life. The positive legacy we will be remembered for. The footprint and impression we will leave behind (or not leave behind).

Defining Statements focus on inclusiveness, collaboration, and support. They are statements that drive us to achieve *better* outcomes, not just *more* outcomes. Outcomes that enrich our own life, *as well as* the lives of others. This may be through improved communications, respectful dealings with others, or leadership that inspires others to greater levels of self-belief and self-acceptance.

The following are some of the *Defining Statements* that I use to guide my behaviours through various situations and scenarios.

Statements that remind me to listen, engage and empathise:

> *'The right word may be effective, but no word was ever as effective as a rightly timed pause.'*

Mark Twain

> *'When you talk, you are only repeating what you already know. But if you listen, you may learn something new.'*
>
> Dali Lama

A statement that guides me in how to educate and inform:

> *'The best teachers are those that show you where to look, but don't tell you what to see.'*
>
> Alexandra K. Trenfor

Removing Rubbish Quotes and Statements

What are some of the "inspirational" quotes and statements you find to be pointless rubbish?

Perhaps they are quotes that make no sense, have been used and abused, or have been morphed to convey a message unrelated to their original intent? Have you used any of these quotes and statements to create goals that should now be re-evaluated?

Defining Quotes and Statements

Now make a list of *Defining Statements* that will inspire you in a constructive and balanced manner.

Ones that define something valuable and beneficial to you – and to others. Statements that will help guide and define how you will lead your life in a rewarding, achievable, and meaningful way.

Chapter 14

Work-Life Balance

What Does this Mean?

As technology blurs the boundary between where work ends, and where life begins, the quest to find a healthy and sustainable balance between the two has become critically important.

However, the relentless pursuit and pressure of *doing more*, *having more* and *achieving more* in all aspects of life has made the successful juggle of everything on our plates an almost insurmountable challenge for too many.

In the past, when we clocked off at the end of the day, the work-clock stopped, and the life-clock switched on. But now we work longer hours. We remain fully connected and plugged into work and social media 24/7. Unless we are highly self-disciplined at flicking the switch off, there is little escape. We must be sufficiently self-disciplined to literally turn off the laptop, phone, or social media – and sufficiently focused to disconnect and stop checking our phone for messages.

But, included in this quest for work-life balance are life coaches and self-help experts who persist in trying to inspire us to do more and take on more. The growing perception is that if we don't cram more into life, and cram it in successfully, then we are failing. As a result, the evolving notion of work-life balance is a combination of multiple channels of pure bullshit. A perfect *bullshit storm* if you will. The relentless focus on more, and the relentless and never-ending merry-go-round of life – be it work or otherwise – is not sustainable. And when supported by the notion of *enough no longer being enough*, it is well near impossible.

It is utterly exhausting to hear what some try to cram into their lives. The majority are determined not to drop any balls in their daily juggling routine, but fail to realise their level of success in each task is waning as fatigue and disillusionment set in.

Do we have the time, the support network, the head space, or even the know-how, to achieve an acceptable level of success in all that we juggle? Can our current goals, demands and approach make the prospects of a successful juggling act at all possible?

And what of the personal cost that this juggling act extracts?

We are not a finite resource. Something at some point must give. But if it is perceived that dropping something out of our lives is a mark of failure, then what is our solution? Simple: we need to challenge advice that leads us to conclude that the solution is to just try harder, be stronger, or just stay positive (*toxic positivity* at is best). This senseless pursuit of work-life balance is more closely aligned to a pursuit of exhaustion. It should be renamed the *Bullshit Juggle*.

In fact, is the concept of achieving work-life balance a misnomer? Can true balance between the two be achieved? It can, but our approach and mindset must first change.

The process of attempting to separate work and life as distinct components to balance is misguided. We are often attempting to separately balance two aspects of life that are closely intertwined and connected. We must instead take a holistic view to create a manageable balance that can be both sustained and enjoyed.

Are Your Goals Wrong?

As a first step, it is time to re-evaluate our current goals and mindset. We need to define each with greater accuracy, and through a lens focused by realistic expectations. This is needed so that we can better encapsulate what success in each component of our lives should look like.

As detailed in Chapter 13, we must assess whether we are attempting to balance a set of SMART goals with realistic expectations. If we are trying to balance a set of competing, ill-considered, ill-conceived and therefore unachievable goals, then no matter how hard we try, balance can't be achieved.

Once we have appropriate and realistic goals in place, we must also evaluate whether all these measures of success are compatible. I have seen too many lives heavy with frustration and exhaustion, stuck in a cycle where the end point is never reached. In such situations, a significant driver is the practice of setting goals for different arenas and aspects of life in complete isolation from one another. There is a lack of consideration from a broader, and all encapsulating, bigger picture perspective. Each goal would be achievable in isolation, but not when collectively worked towards in conjunction with all other goals.

Of course, there are also those goals set in line with the 'aiming for the stars' and 'just dream it' mentality – driven by pearls of wisdom (bullshit) dropped on us by others, who then up and walk away. Job done. I inspired you. Now you work out the details.

Goals created on the basis of poor advice must be challenged and reviewed as a priority. They must be replaced with SMART goals.

Do Your Resources Match the Need?

I have listened to many, many cries for help to reduce stress levels. People with lives piled high with demands, expectations, and commitments, but where nothing was negotiable for removal or reassessment.

It wouldn't take long to identify the extent of overloading. Aiming to be that extraordinarily successful employee who exceeds all demands and expectations. Being that amazing parent who never misses a school concert, sports event or scraped knee. All while consistently posting on social media to demonstrate how perfect life is, and how much of a kick-arse superstar they are in all aspects of life.

For many, this is not sustainable. But worse – for many it is unattainable. We simply don't have the resources at our disposal.

Sadly, some will even present a contrived perfect life on social media that hides the truth – that they are struggling. Unfortunately, this false portrayal feeds an ongoing negative cycle. We see others portray a perfect life on social media, so we edit and filter our own lives to portray the same – all the while adding further to the pressure of expectation for others to meet another standard that is also false.

The outcome – how many of the perfect lives portrayed on media are false and contrived to some degree? We will perhaps never know, but we will more likely know the pressure felt attempting to engineer a life the same – to achieve what others appear to be so successfully achieving.

Several years ago, I listened to a presenter speak to a group of senior female professionals. The topic: how to successfully be an amazing star at work and an amazing parent at home. There were many great little nuggets of advice: tips, tricks and insights. All great ideas on how to simultaneously achieve success at work and at home.

But, as I listened, I could not hear the big-ticket item that enabled the presenter to manage all in her life so successfully. It all just seemed too much to manage.

But right at the very end the kicker came:

> *'If it weren't for our live-in nanny, I don't know how we would manage.'*

There it was. The truth. This person lacked the resources, so had outsourced key tasks to a live-in nanny. It was the most significant factor but mentioned fleetingly as an aside.

An 'Oh, by the way' snippet thrown in at the very end.

But how did outsourcing to the nanny back up comments that had also been made regarding being a present, and always-there-for-everything parent, when half of everything was being outsourced to said nanny?

Not everyone has a home large enough, nor pockets deep enough, to employ a live-in nanny. Nor do all of us want to.

Achieving work-life balance will often require something to give. Something let go, or goals reassessed; perhaps permanently, perhaps just for the foreseeable future, and under the current circumstances.

Unfortunately, too many role models convey that you can 'have your cake and eat it too.' But be careful. Are they accurately portraying the *whole* truth of the matter? Alternatively, have they secretly employed a chef who cooks the cake, serves the cake and then washes up after? Their only task: open mouth and chew. Easy.

But there are sure to be social media posts where that amazing "homemade" cake is held up for all to see. And here, we make incorrect assumptions that it was all their own doing. Subsequently, we risk feelings of guilt or inferiority if we can't achieve the same. And if we aren't careful, we fall prey to feelings of an *Imposter Syndrome*.

We then exhaust ourselves trying to achieve the same, all while being influenced by incomplete messages. Intentional or not, we are deceived.

Now that is bullshit!

Celebrate the Journey – Not Just the Arrival

Another burden in the work-life juggle routine is an excessive focus on where we need to get to, and what is yet to be done. The focus becomes 'are we there yet, are we there yet?'

Our perspective is therefore frequently rooted into looking towards the future. Specifically, it is often fixated on what remains to be completed, achieved, finished, or ticked off our to-do list. The result is an excessive amount of time spent focusing on what lays ahead, and insufficient time spent reflecting on what we have already achieved.

Looking back at what we have accomplished provides motivation to keep moving forward. Looking backward also presents ample opportunities to recognise what we have learnt, and how we have grown.

A key enabler to assist us manage our balance, and find our personal sweet spot, is remaining motivated. The feeling that we are making progress is a powerful motivator. To experience the positive feelings created by getting things done and improving from where we started.

Solely fixating on our destination point, and the journey that remains ahead, detracts from both appreciating how far we have progressed, and appreciating the journey as it unfolds.

How can we put in perspective where we are headed, if we have not understood where we have come from?

As the Danish philosopher Kierkegaard said:

> 'Life can only be understood backwards; but it must be lived forwards.'
>
> Soren Kierkegaard

Chapter 15

The Alternative - Finding Your Personal Sweet Spot

Recalibrate Your Focus

A sound starting point for finding a healthier work-life balance is to recalibrate our focus.

To achieve a better balance between looking forward at where we are heading and looking back to appreciate the journey of where we have come from. To consider Kierkegaard's words so that we find enjoyment in living our life, but also realise understanding to grow and develop.

An excessive forward focused perspective can miss opportunities for reflective growth and self-discovery, while an excessive backward focused perspective can cause us to be weighed down and restricted by our past experiences and learnings. Particularly, by those events that are highly negative and toxic.

In the following diagrams, the thickness of the curved arrows represents the amount of time we spend adopting forward-orientated and backward-orientated perspectives. The thicker the line the greater the focus.

A poorly balanced forward perspective is represented in the first diagram. This is where we spend an excessive amount of time ruminating on what we have not achieved, and how much remains to be done before we reach our goals. Little time is spent looking back to learn and appreciate how we have progressed.

The outcome can be exhaustion as we are in a constant state of working to move forward and achieve. If we aren't careful, it can create a sense of never arriving, as there will always be another goal, another target and another need to satisfy.

As presented in the second diagram, an excessive focus on the past is also not balanced. An excess focus of this type can lead to past experiences becoming weights that hold us down and hold as back from moving forward.

An excessive focus on the past can also result in an inability to learn from our experiences and grow. Therefore, our ability to set new and constructive goals is hampered as we become stuck in the past.

The third diagram represents a shift to a healthy and balanced perspective. A balanced perspective is where we reflect sufficiently on what we have *already* achieved, what we have *already* learnt, and the growth *already* realised.

It looks at the past to recognise and appreciate growth, and to feel a sense of movement forward. It is not looking at the past to fixate on failings or toxic events.

A future focused perspective still exists as we work towards our clearly defined goals and aspirations. But exhaustion is less likely as we also pause frequently to celebrate our successes.

Only then do we set off again toward our next goal, but now instilled with a sense of satisfaction from our accomplishments.

POORLY BALANCED FORWARD PERSPECTIVE

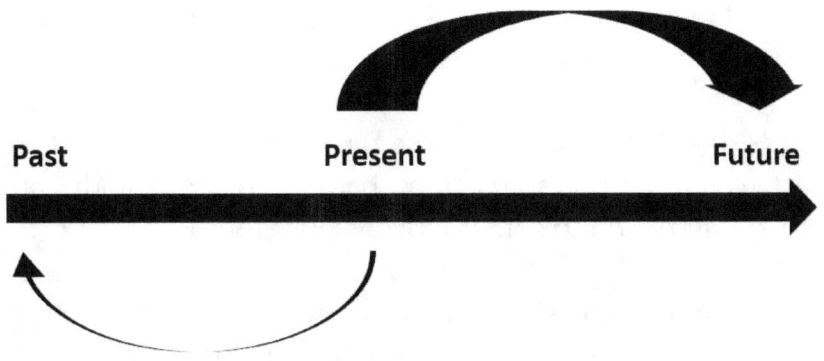

POORLY BALANCED BACKWARD PERSPECTIVE

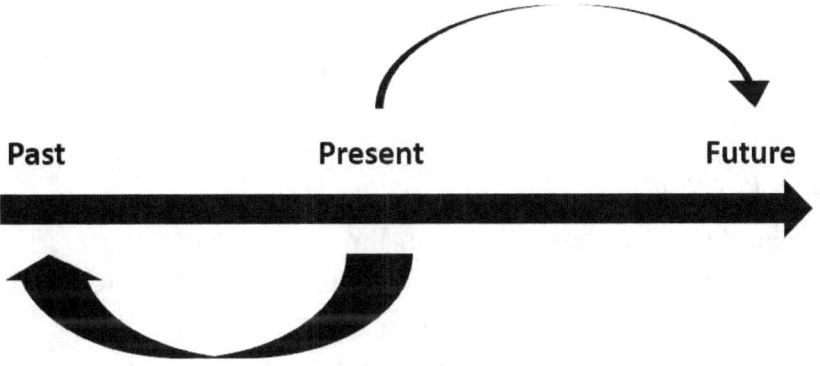

BALANCED PERSPECTIVE

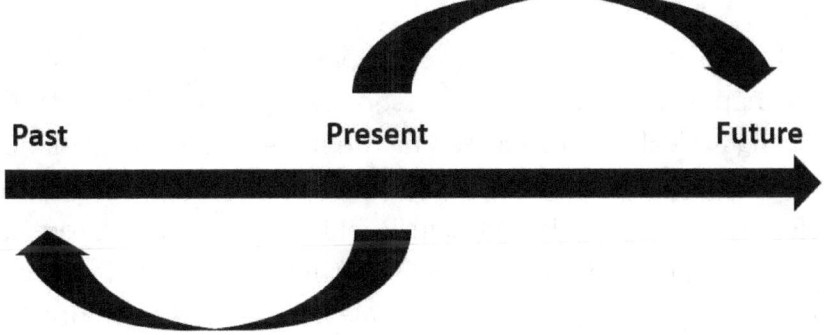

Reviewing Your Perspective

Take time to assess the balance of your current perspective to determine if change is necessary.

Is it overly biased toward the past or the future? Are there past experiences that must be better processed and learnt from to allow you to constructively move forward?

Is there an excessive fixation on the future that is causing fatigue and restricting your ability to learn from the past? Do you take the time needed to pause, reflect, and celebrate your successes and achievements?

It is up to *you* which perspective to choose.

It's Personal

Finding the right balance in life is a personal matter. This may seem like an over-simplistic statement of the obvious, but in much of the advice I have read, and had shared with me over the years, this is frequently not what is disseminated.

Instead, there is a plethora of advice that tells us precisely what a successful balance between areas such as our work and home life *must* look like. Clear directions on what it *must* include.

I have had countless conversations with people exceptionally happy with their own personally created balance, while having to deal with others telling them the mix of their balance was in need of recalibration. Not enough work and too much life, or vice versa. Not enough hobbies, not enough exercise, not enough holidays. But much of this work-life balance advice is only suitable for some, while being completely unsuitable to others. A personal solution is always needed.

When I started *Bramwell Solutions* I was given countless tips on how to create routines and habits that would assist me shift from a home mindset to a work mindset each morning – a particularly important topic given I would be working from a home office.

Creating routines and habits is critical, but one piece of advice was easy to ignore. I was told the key to success was dressing each morning in my work attire of suit and tie (which, you may recall, was something I wanted to avoid), jump in my car, drive around the neighbourhood and park back in my garage. But, I was to imagine I had just pulled into the carpark of my corporate office. With this approach I was guaranteed an immediate transition to a "work mindset." I'd be ready to work. My productivity would skyrocket.

This advice was delivered with earnest intent. Maybe it works for some. But for me it would have just been a pointless waste of time and effort. Personally, I work equally well in tracksuit pants!

My Personal Balance

I most definitely don't want to add additional bullshit to the work-life balance equation. Instead, I will simply share the three critical questions I use to challenge my coaching participants to consider whether a suitable personal balance has been found between their work and life.

If the answer to any of these three questions is no, then a rethink might be necessary.

1. Is it sustainable?

If the answer is yes, then brilliant. You have a balance that is not excessively focused on a specific area of life. Your personal balance should be maintainable over the foreseeable future. If no, then something needs to give. Is it reduced work hours?

Reduced intensity? Or perhaps a better balance of other life pursuits to create broader harmony in life? Perhaps more pursuits beyond work? Perhaps less?

2. Is it enjoyable?

We can't all have careers and life endeavours that solely connect to higher-level drivers and motivators, but we can all try to find employment that is sufficiently enjoyable to allow us appreciation of other areas of life. When our work creates high levels of irritation, it becomes difficult to enjoy anything else life offers. It is then that the frustrations, boredom or stress of work-life infects *all* aspects of life.

Therefore, if the answer to this question is no, with broader impact across other life components, then change is critical.

3. Does it do no harm?

If the answer is yes, then sustaining and maintaining the enjoyment of your work-life balance is yours to be had. But be wary. This question can be difficult to answer correctly. We aren't always aware when harm is occurring to our mental and physical well-being until well into a harm cycle. We may think the answer is yes, but be completely unaware of the building side effects of overwork, stress, or boredom.

Therefore, if the answer is no, then change is warranted to protect long-term mental and/or physical health.

Clearly these questions are neither a complete, nor perfect, self-assessment of our work-life balance mix. As I have stated, attaining work-life balance is personal. What I have personally settled on as the right mix for *my* life and *my* circumstances may indeed be viewed by some as lazy, and by others as excessive. These three questions should be used to begin a healthy, and perhaps much needed, process of self-reflection. One single 'no' response may balance out two strong 'yes' responses.

But beware of the 'no' responses, for experience tells me that the future may not be looking as bright without some degree of change.

Reviewing Your Balance

Evaluate your current work-life balance against each of these three questions. Are all your answers 'yes'?

Can you identify any possible need for change? Are there any 'no' responses that necessitate the need for immediate reflection and change?

A Holistic Perspective

My own personal and professional focus is to build a sustainable consulting business that provides beneficial outcomes to my clients. I have no grand plans to build a massive consulting empire. I have no desire to build a huge team to spread the *Bramwell Solutions* philosophy. In fact, if I were aiming for these things it would be in direct opposition to why *Bramwell Solutions* was born. It would be counterproductive to what I have set as my own personal goals. Goals that take a holistic view of my own life, and all that hold great importance to me.

Bramwell Solutions' Balanced Goal Scorecard

When *Bramwell Solutions* was born I developed a *Balanced Goal Scorecard* approach to define and guide my behaviours across all facets of my life.

To this day, this approach continues to allow me to find my own personal sweet spot – my own personal balance in all areas of life.

What follows is what I developed. It's for *me*. It may not suit you. But sharing it may help you commence a process of evaluating the suitability of your current goals.

1. Client focus

- Delivery of high-quality services in areas of my core expertise
- Being the trusted advisor in my areas of core expertise
- Providing solutions that have high impact and sustained benefit
- Providing pro bono offerings to not for profit organisations.

2. Financial focus

- Sustainable service growth year on year
- Diversification of service offerings to existing clients
- Leveraging existing experiences to expand into diverse industries and sectors
- Revenue growth through client referral and recommendations.

3. Family

- Being a present and highly participative parent
- Being seen by my children as a primary person for care and support
- Providing enriching life experiences
- Being truly present at key development events and celebrations.

4. Self

- Providing consulting services that I'm passionate about
- Working with a diversity of clients that gives me personal satisfaction
- Managing stressors and work-life balance to support a healthy lifestyle
- Remaining committed to ongoing personal and professional development.

Over the years I have used these points to make short-term and long-term decisions about the direction of *Bramwell Solutions*. They have acted as my compass to determine and define my specific targets and next steps.

Using this approach allows me to live the key messages delivered through my consulting services: building people-centric leadership practices and workplace cultures that embrace and support diversity, inclusion, and creativity.

And as surmised perfectly by the American poet and author Maya Angelou:

> 'Success is liking yourself, liking what you do, and liking how you do it.'

Maya Angelou

And with this approach, I personally have a resounding sense of success!

One Critical Measure Above all Others

When my first child was born, two years after starting *Bramwell Solutions*, I added one additional success measure. It was a higher-level overarching measure that could only be met as a by-product of successfully performing in a manner aligned with my balanced scorecard. If I was not meeting this overarching measure, then it would give pause for thought to reassess whether I was truly behaving in a way that was aligned with my goals:

> *When my son is hurt, he will readily come to me for comfort and support.*

I know this sounds simplistic, perhaps corny to some. But hear me out.

If my son were hurt, and he came to me as readily as he came to my wife for comfort and support, I felt it would signify the following three things were happening:

- I was happy and approachable because I was enjoying my work
- I wasn't stressed as my work was both intellectually and financially rewarding
- I was present (both mentally and physically) to build a strong bond with my son by managing my work and home life successfully.

It has been insightful over the years to share this key measure with others and observe their reactions. Some have perceived it to be unprofessional – lacking sufficient business focus. Where were my key growth targets? While others have found it to be exceptionally thought provoking, with some even telling me it had prompted a reassessment of their own goals and measures of success.

Personally, this overarching measure is exactly what I wanted. It is exceptionally personal, and it encompasses precisely why I set up my own business. It encompasses perfectly what I aim to achieve. It is a significant driver of the work-life balance I personally want.

In the ensuing years there has only been one tweak to this measure, to ensure it continued to remain relevant and accurately reflected my life:

> *When my son or daughter is hurt, he/she will readily come to me for comfort and support.*

Creating Goals and Measures that are Meaningful to You

What would your *Balanced Goal Scorecard* look like?

What parts of your life would be featured? How would you define and assess your own personal measure(s) of success?

Part 3: Specific Areas Abundant with Bullshit

Areas where bullshit advice and bullshit habits have become the norm to create dysfunctional and poor practices.

Chapter 16

The Over-Complication of Leadership

The Impact of a Great Leader

Leadership is without doubt one of the most widely researched and written about topics of today.

Academics, researchers and consultants worldwide continue to define what great leadership does and doesn't entail. Are we born as great leaders, or do we become great leaders? Nature versus nurture, and so on.

The influence and impact of a leader on the success of an individual, a team, and an organisation is undisputedly massive. The impact of a great leader on their community, country, and the world immeasurable. While the impact of a poor leader can be catastrophic and soul-destroying.

Unfortunately, there is also an abundance of gimmicky fads and tips that erroneously define what a great leader should or should not be doing. Tips that were relevant to a specific scenario, but then incorrectly extrapolated across many other scenarios or situations for which they were never intended, or to which they simply don't apply. Tips that may provide immediate gain, but come with longer-term complications. And of course, tips that are just plain nonsensical bullshit that unfortunately sell.

There are the ideas that were relevant at a specific point in time, that challenged thinking and evolved leadership practices out of the dark ages. But now, no longer apply. Those that are well past their use-by date, that urgently need to be graciously retired or thrown out. While there are others that should never have been suggested in the first place.

My Leadership Bullshit Hit List

For a leader to be successful, they must be skilled at discerning between sound and valid leadership practices, and the latest gimmicky tips and ideas that don't achieve sustainable improvements in leadership performance.

The following are a few of the tips and ideas that I have encountered over the years that make my personal leadership bullshit hitlist. Misguided, ill-informed or outdated pieces of advice that need to be critically challenged, closely scrutinised, or (in many cases) simply thrown away. Advice that causes confusion, damage, and a senseless waste of resource (time, money and effort) in both their pursuit and their use.

1. My door is always open' policy

This is the classic leadership policy used to portray a leader who is always available and accessible. A leader who is open, approachable, and who can be always be trusted to be supportive. But it's bullshit.

If we genuinely feel the need to make this statement, and actually leave our office door open, then we are clearly missing the mark regarding how to effectively convey our "approachability." An open-door policy frequently conveys nothing that resembles anything close to approachability.

Too often it plays out in other toxic ways: *'It's open so that you can feel free to come in and be yelled at to go away'* policy. *'I have decided to enable everyone to come to me with everything trivial that they should be discussing with someone else'* policy. Or my personal favourite: *'I can't get anything done, because you keep coming into my office'* policy.

A door being physically open doesn't convey approachability. Approachability is the sum of all our actions as a leader. Actions of empathy, individualised consideration to understand a team member's blockers to success, or accurately recognising an individual's strengths and weaknesses to work with.

It is the ongoing supportive and authentic dialogue that signifies the door is open. Not the actual door itself!

2. Treating employees like family

I understand where this notion comes from. But it can create immense problems and guilt for leaders when managing organisational change, or when managing employee performance.

The intent is to challenge leaders and their organisations to view employees as people. For staff to be seen as individuals to support and empathise with, like one would with a family member. To treat staff as a valuable resource, not simply as a dispensable commodity. The notion being that if a family member let us down, we wouldn't kick them out of the family. No way. Instead, we would counsel them, teach them, develop them, nurture them and support them to improve – no matter what it takes.

But our employees are *not* part of our family. They do not want to be – nor should be – treated in a child-like or paternal manner. If all exhaustive performance management efforts fail, and they still can't meet expected standards, then they should be removed. This may sound harsh, but failure to do so disrespects every other employee. Someone else must pick up the slack. Other employees will perceive that poor performance (or attitude) is condoned. Inequality and a lack of fairness will be perceived. Different levels of accountability and performance expectations will appear to exist across an organisation.

There is also the stark reality that an individual employee is part of a larger entity. An entity whose ongoing viability and success benefits all employees, owners, customers and stakeholders. To treat each team member as family is misguided. It risks the benefit of all for the over-protection of one.

And what of the underperforming team member held onto as "family"? Kept in a role where they are in a constant state of struggle, or where they lack the required skills and abilities to perform effectively. This represents a great disservice to the individual. And it's an exceptionally demotivating place to be.

Assisting an employee to identify opportunities for which they are better suited is one of the greatest acts of compassionate leadership that one can display. A true leader is one who can empathetically and constructively convey the reality of a difficult situation – no bullshit.

That is a leader to trust.

I have seen many dysfunctional and misguided attempts at "leading a family" that have simply become an excuse for inaction. Where instead, it acted as a reason to avoid making the hard decisions. The reality is that poor performing staff use up valuable resources that could be better spent elsewhere developing others. Ignoring and not rectifying sustained and entrenched poor performance, will almost always result in significant negative impacts on other team members.

To convey authentic leadership, and a fair and equitable workplace culture, we must be prepared to make tough staffing calls – but only once all rocks have been turned over, and all options exhausted.

> *Treat employees with respect, with uniformity of expectation and with strong support.*

Don't treat them as dispensable. But equally, *don't* treat them as family.

3. Expecting people to always go above and beyond

Once expected and agreed standards of performance and goals have been set, it's simply ludicrous to then expect (or in some instances even demand) staff to go above and beyond these goals. Unfortunately, these absurd goal-setting habits are happening with such increasing frequency, that the actual goal set is often not the real goal at all. It is now commonly accepted that only those that exceed goals will gain high praise and recognition.

The pressure and strain that this places on an individual can be huge. Again, remember the concept of *enough no longer being enough*?

There are several drivers behind this mindset. It could be an out of control and rampant expectation of more. It could be a lack of leadership and communication skills to effectively articulate goals that fully challenge the individual in the first place. It could even be a lack of planning to effectively forecast and identify organisation goals or team goals that can be effectively translated into meaningful individual goals.

But ultimately, it appears to be driven by our insatiable appetite for more. Enough!

If an individual, team or organisation goes above and beyond what was asked, it is a bonus. For the rest who meet their defined goals, they should be regarded as successfully achieving exactly what was asked.

Those who meet their defined goals must also be highly praised. Praise must not be reserved for only those who exceed.

And if the goals were incorrectly set from the outset, it is the leader's and organisation's issue to address. Goals must always be set at a level at which their successful completion will be sufficiently noteworthy to celebrate. It is not the follower's responsibility to rectify poorly set goals that are subsequently deemed to be too easy to achieve.

4. 'Great leaders are great coaches' mantra

Sure, this mantra can be correct. Great leaders *do* typically have superior coaching skills. But that is only part of the repertoire of a great leader.

The idea of "leader as a coach" has grown without a balanced perspective to accompany it. A leader who coaches is one who guides, who questions, who nurtures and who constructively challenges. These are all exceptional leadership traits.

But the concept of a "coaching leader" has become grossly overused. The result is the development of leaders who lack the skills, appreciate the need, or recognise the moment, where effective and appropriate delegation, or clear and decisive direction, are the best courses of action.

Delegation opportunities are missed or ignored as the leader continues the idea of coaching by checking in to see how the team or individual is doing. The outcome is excessive "just checking-in" and monitoring of behaviours and performance.

> *Any form of leadership that is in excess of the approach required is a form of micromanaging.*

An overly biased focus on coaching also creates leaders who don't correctly identify key moments where strong, decisive, and clear direction are required. Situations that necessitate strong and decisive leadership can suffer, as the leader asks for input when instead urgency is critical. Key deadlines that demand decisiveness are missed as individuals and teams go round and round in circles A leadership rudder is lacking to provide clear input and guidance.

Therefore, a great leader *is* a great coach. But a great leader is *also* a great delegator *and* a great director of action. They correctly recognise the right moment for each leadership style. They correctly recognise when a situational shift requires a re-think or change in approach.

Challenging Poor Leadership

I've witnessed many great leaders engage and inspire their staff to achieve amazing outcomes. Unfortunately, I have also witnessed leadership practices that have been negligent and harmful.

I've helped employees cope with the ramifications of leadership styles that lacked a nurturing or supportive focus. I have helped employees remain resilient when leaders appeared intent on creating obstacles to success. I've observed environments where the proactive stifling of personal growth and development were common practice.

Unfortunately, it is incredibly difficult to motivate a dysfunctional leader to change their stripes, particularly when they feel they are embracing a style that is regarded as their personal recipe for success. There can be an inability to identify the limitations of their current style, and an unwillingness to recognise that they will go no further without change.

When an individual is so entrenched in their habits that they are unable, or unwilling, to see their leadership flaws or shortcomings, it can be necessary to introduce a simple paradigm shift. To propose a different perspective to help prise their eyes open and see the world differently.

For example, to challenge a leader to view their style and delivery as though they were parenting techniques. Would statement X or action Y appropriately support the development of a young child into a healthy and high-functioning adult? An adult with high self-esteem and a thirst for growth and development? If the answer is no, then why use the same style of delivery to an adult, and still expect them to develop and perform well?

Of course, some leaders fail to see the shortcomings and flaws inherent in their actions. These are the leaders that are the hardest to challenge and change. These are the leaders that are often blissfully ignorant with low self-awareness. And these are the leaders that concern me greatly.

Why? Because these same leaders can be so high in self-confidence that they are the ones most adept at selling themselves as "experts" and becoming leadership coaches. They impart onto others their pearls of wisdom and secrets for leadership success.

But be wary. These are neither pearls of wisdom nor secrets I recommend you learn.

Getting it Wrong

Years ago, I experienced an organisation where leadership "experts" were everywhere. In fact, this organisation appeared to grow them on trees. Many were very keen to tell me how great they were as leaders. But one thing I have learnt over the years – a great leader doesn't tell you how great *they* are. They tell you how great their *staff* are.

On one occasion, I was invited into an "expert's" office so that he could expound his greatness as a leader, communicator and content matter expert. What followed was detailed bragging about attendance at leadership courses and seminars run by world leading universities. I heard about his leadership philosophy, how he created great followers, and his personal snapshot of what he believed made a genuinely great leader. All traits and attributes that he of course had an overflowing abundance of.

However, this entire speech was delivered with the "expert's" feet firmly planted on his desk – directly in front of me. Eye contact could only be achieved by me shifting in my seat and stretching my neck to see past the soles of his shoes.

My takeaway from listening to this "expert" in action? Despite all his high-level theory and ideas on leadership, he was devoid of fundamental traits of respect and decency. This supposedly exceptional leader was highly educated and intelligent, but seriously lacking in the qualities essential for basic, let alone expert, leadership.

It doesn't matter what fancy course we have been to, or what letters we have after our name. It certainly doesn't matter how many years we have worked as a leader.

It all comes down to core and fundamental interactions that do, or do not, build authenticity, trust and respect. This is what leadership is all about in its most simple form. Respecting and inspiring people in a manner that best supports *them* to succeed.

Leadership "Experts"

The definition of expertise encompasses words such as skill, competence, prowess, professionalism and mastery. Therefore, the "expert" is a master of their profession. They possess a level of prowess that places them at the pinnacle of their field.

But how do we determine the existence of expertise? How do we determine who is, or isn't, a so-called "expert"?

Within a sporting context this is simple. There are rankings, awards and championships. These are typically determined by a peak body that clearly defines the criteria of expertise by the laws and rules of the game and the tournaments played. Those at the top are the absolute benchmark of expertise.

But what of a business context? In the business world, so called "experts" appear to have been breeding at a ferocious rate. Look around and we can see them everywhere. But how? Is it because we are all 'aiming for the stars,' and greater numbers of people previously considered "average" have taken that next step to "expertness"? Or is it simply the notion of being an "expert" has become a term anyone can claim on their LinkedIn profile or flash looking business card? Unfortunately, it appears to be the latter. Individuals who have had some degree of success in one business area, then extrapolate that success across numerous other areas – many tenuously related at best.

I have listened to self-proclaimed leadership "experts" tout cringeworthy and harmful advice. I have listened as they postulate and pontificate how their own personal brand of leadership had created amazing workplace cultures. Yet, these cultures were dysfunctional. Cultures where staff were apprehensive and scared to share ideas or provide feedback. Cultures where the leader's idea of "constructive feedback" amounted to nothing better than harassment and persecution. I have then watched on with horror as some of these leaders embarked on consulting careers, intent on teaching others the secrets to their success.

We must be careful not to blindly give value to messages that come from self-proclaimed expertise. We must critically analyse and review information to effectively judge its merit and value. To also judge information independent of its source.

We need to remove bullshit from the leadership development dialogue.

A Reminder – Don't Always Trust an "Expert"

Several years ago, I had the pleasure of observing a self-proclaimed leadership "expert" in action.

I was facilitating a mentoring program with a group of senior female leaders – each with exceptionally strong skills, experiences, and qualifications. One session included a guest speaker. A master executive coach who claimed to 'teach coaches how to coach.' A self-proclaimed expert in career planning, career growth, and with a core focus on developing exceptional leaders. A true "expert" in his trade.

He commenced his session with a short questionnaire. The responses would apparently help him to better understand the obstacles that stood before each of these very senior female professionals.

However, the questionnaire included a series of highly sexist questions, along the lines of: 'Do you find having to make dinner at night for your children holds back your career growth?' 'Do morning school drop-offs limit your ability to be present at work?'

A simple test of whether a question is sexist, is whether it would be asked equally of both genders, if at all. These questions were "designed" for women. So, yes. They were sexist!

Once his "expert eye" had reviewed the responses, he stepped to the whiteboard. From this position of authority, he proceeded to draw a simple quadrant with two variables: Introvert and Extrovert. He then boldly declared that, as women, they were all introverts who needed to build their confidence to effectively express their opinions.

WHAT? Based on what? How? Why?

Oh, the countless ways in which this "expert" was wrong. Sexist and gross generalisations. Ill-informed analysis. And a poor appreciation of what introversion alludes to.

And what did a background review of this expert "coach of coaches" reveal? No qualifications, no grounding, and no experience in human behaviour. Instead, a former finance executive who self-proclaimed he knew the secrets to leadership success.

What damage would this "expert" cause when coaching – particularly to the self-esteem of women? What havoc and destruction would be caused to his clients' goals and aspirations?

But this situation also taught me a valuable lesson. Always carefully vet your guest speakers!

Chapter 17

The Alternative - Authentic Leadership

Individualised Consideration

As opposed to following the latest set of gimmicky leadership fads and trends, we need to create authentic leadership.

Leadership that encapsulates doing what is *right*. It might be hard to achieve, it may take focused effort, and it may include unpopular decisions – but an authentic leader should have a moral compass that aims for *right*.

Individualised Consideration is a key component of authentic leadership. It is the notion of understanding the relevant skills, abilities, and experiences of each team member or follower in detail. Only then do we set goals, design career paths, or explore development strategies that are targeted accordingly to each. It is this consideration that also enables us to know what is right.

This approach is equally applicable across a range of contexts – be it business, leisure, sporting or otherwise. It challenges the 'one size fits all' approach. It drives a dynamic and fluid leadership style that constructively challenges and supports the growth of the individual. Each and every single one.

Inspiring leaders understand every team member or follower's specific motivators, drivers, and inhibitors to sustained effective performance. Without this level of detailed and specific insight, effective engagement and connection with the individual, and consequently broader teams, is severely hampered.

Leaders who recognise the value of *Individualised Consideration,* will question, listen, and seek deeper understanding of the individual sitting before them. One-on-one conversations include core questions such as: 'What do you need from me to succeed?' 'What obstacles can I work with you to remove?' 'How can I support your success?'

Authentic Leadership

So how do we become authentic leaders? There are several core elements all great leaders possess. Get these core elements right, and you will have in place the foundations from which to grow and develop into a truly authentic leader.

Most importantly, they are also the elements that will support followers to thrive and succeed. But these elements are not only unique to the authentic and trustworthy leader. They are also the domain of authentic and trustworthy people: community members, teammates, parents, partners and more.

1. Create a safe learning environment

Firstly, create a safe learning environment that is free from ambiguity caused by shifting rules, ambiguous expectations, and political game play.

A critical component is setting clear expectations and boundaries that contain sufficiently detailed information. This will assist individuals effectively self-regulate. It provides clarity around what is *within bounds* and what is *out of bounds*. Then, with this heightened clarity in place, grant people the autonomy and latitude to operate with independence within this safe and supportive environment.

Allow them to take appropriate risks, step outside their comfort zone, and challenge themselves to go further than they may have originally imagined possible. But this growth is not pushed by unrealistic and 'more' oriented mantras. It is fostered by creating a sense of psychological safety. Clarity that shortcomings or failures will not be met with punishment and retribution. Clarity that the focus lies firmly on learning, developing, and supporting personal growth.

2. Accept mistakes as a given

Refusing to accept mistakes as a natural component of innovation and growth stifles creativity. It also strengthens the individual's dependence on the leader to provide direction and creative input.

If mistakes are used as an opportunity to punish rather than develop, then personal development, autonomy and drive will all suffer. An authentic leader must demonstrate calmness and tolerance as individuals embark on their personal journey of trial and error, while they assimilate and bed down new ideas, or discover new ways. A great leader is supportive and available during the hard times, and fans the flames of creativity during times of stagnation.

Critically, a great leader must also assist and facilitate ongoing constructive self-reflection and learning.

3. Provide immediate feedback

Don't wait until that monthly catch up, or even worse the yearly performance review discussion to provide feedback. Providing immediate feedback tightens the feedback loop and supports instantaneous modification of strategies and approaches. Creating a culture of immediate and constructive feedback encourages the individual to frequently critique their own work. Immediate and constructive feedback speeds up growth. It strengthens feelings of positive self-esteem and accomplishment, as shifts in behaviour and improved output are achieved.

Feedback must be provided that is focused on growth and learning. It should never be biased towards a process of punishment and retribution. Feedback must be delivered assertively and empathetically. This will ensure messages resonate, and shift performance for the better.

4. Lavish unconditional praise for effort

Praise must be heartfelt and genuine. Never combine praise with poorly attempted negative criticism.

We must avoid the 'Oh, that was fantastic, but next time you should...' type of statements. These statements serve only to turn positive praise into the precursor of a knock down.

Praise must stand-alone. No conditions. No provisos. No buts.

Just a statement that conveys genuine, clear, and honest appreciation of a job well done. The recognition of effort that extended and challenged the individual to step out of their comfort zone, or to precisely deliver what was required.

A simple 'thank you' is a powerful statement.

It is also important to ensure praise isn't focused on outcomes alone. It must encompass the effort demonstrated to achieve (or even at times, to not achieve) the result.

Work by American psychologist Caroline Dweck defined the benefit derived from developing a *Growth Mindset*. This mindset is developed when the encouragement and praise of effort translates into a greater willingness to take appropriate risks and take on greater challenges. A *Growth Mindset* drives a learning-oriented perspective, where achieving the perfect result is not the only measure of success. Success is also measured by the level of *effort*.

However, according to Dweck's work, focusing on outcomes alone creates a *Fixed Mindset*. Here the individual stays in their comfort zone and sticks to tasks they feel certain can be successfully completed, as this will earn outcome focused praise. The result? Development is stifled.

With a *Fixed Mindset,* tasks that may extend the individual's skills and knowledge are avoided – they present a possibility for failure. Therefore, the *Fixed Mindset* individual focuses on task they feel certain, and able, to successfully complete to gain praise. They avoid tasks that may stretch their skills and abilities, and which likely carry greater risk that a successful outcome will not occur. The outcome: they *play it safe*.

5. Act as a role model

Finally – be what we would have others be. Don't confuse role modelling with a rolling up of the sleeves and getting your hands dirty in the trenches.

Instead, it is about role modelling the *values*, the *mindset* and the *behaviours* that support others to know precisely how to act when their leader is not watching. To understand right from wrong. To differentiate between correct focus and dedication, from distraction and undesirable tangents.

Followers need to understand and appreciate what success looks and feels like. What they should aspire to emulate must be clearly visible through the daily behaviours of their authentic leader.

Appreciate the Expertise Around You

To support leadership growth, it is also important to not ignore the talented individuals and amazing ideas that might be right under our nose. At times, we can learn valuable leadership lessons from some of the most unlikely sources.

Just because someone doesn't proclaim to know it all, or have 100,000 followers on Twitter, doesn't mean they lack valuable insights and ideas worth sharing and listening to. Again, don't judge the quality of an idea by its source alone. Judge it on its merits.

We are often challenged to look beyond our network and current spheres of influence to find new solutions and improved approaches. But what if we first looked more closely within our current networks. We may discover unrealised and unearthed creativity and brilliance that is right before us.

I see the opposite all the time. A prominent CEO or business guru shares their sage piece of advice, and we quickly adapt our behaviour and promote the advice as a "game changer." But then an "unknown" presents the exact same message, we don't place the same value on it. Instead, we too readily pass it off as ill-informed or naïve, and not really "getting it."

Great leaders listen better to those around them. They non-judgementally open their eyes and ears to see and hear all the potential value and insights that might otherwise be missed.

I challenge you. Go unearth a moment of brilliance staring you in the face. It could be someone sitting across from you on the train or sitting in your next meeting. It could be someone holding onto an unrealised game changer. It could be an opinion that points out a flaw in the information used to determine your current path.

Becoming an Authentic and Inspirational Leader

Consider my leadership "hit list" outlined at the start of this chapter, and the foundations for leadership success.

Do you agree? How do you feel you compare against these? Do you have any habits that should be removed?

Consider the different core elements of leadership. In what ways must you change?

Being More Critical

What leadership ideas, opinions and advice do you need to critically challenge? What concepts do you need to re-evaluate and apply a critical assessment?

Are you receptive to hearing and seeing brilliance, irrespective of its source?

Chapter 18

Lack of Responsiveness

An Outcome of the Focus on More

There are numerous observable symptoms of bullshit: high workloads, excessive work-life demands, and a biased focus on meeting our own needs.

Another concerning outcome is a decline in levels of responsiveness. Communications, biased toward seeking first to be understood, as opposed to seeking first to understand, will result in too much time and effort being placed on making requests, and insufficient time and effort placed on responding to requests.

Consequently, a disrespectful communication profile is created, where we appear to place little value on the needs of others. And, if external self-awareness is low, we create a blind spot in which we unknowingly frustrate others as we fail to follow up on requests received, fail to finish a dialogue or discussion started, or fail to convey a clear opinion when asked.

It is Bad for Your Brand

Let me make something clear. Ignoring someone is not the same as saying no. Not responding and not finishing an interaction is bullshit.

I'm not referring to unsolicited annoying approaches where, out of the blue, a stranger attempts to sell us something we neither asked for, nor wanted. We should feel free to ignore these unsolicited approaches.

No, I'm referring to interactions where we made the initial approach. We asked a question but didn't acknowledge the response. We didn't finish the conversation. We didn't indicate our intent. We didn't even acknowledge the effort.

Maybe our question only required a simple answer. Maybe it required much running around, research and time. Time – that resource we never have enough of, and we just used it up for someone else.

To ignore someone with whom we initiated contact is unforgivable. Further, to ignore a response to a question we asked is incredibly damaging to our personal brand. It speaks volumes. But it speaks volumes we don't want to convey.

It risks insinuating we don't respect others. It suggests we simply feel our time is more valuable than the time of others. Alternatively, it may also provide a sense that we are poorly organised. None of these are good for our personal, or professional, brands.

> *One of the biggest side effects of a lack of responsiveness is the festering of negative emotions.*

This can take the form of growing resentment, frustration, and annoyance caused by our lack of respectful communication. Again, all emotions that we should do our best to avoid creating and feeding.

Whatever the personal driver, the reality is that the unrelenting focus on more makes it increasingly difficult to manage all our interactions effectively. We are juggling multiple demands that are often competing for the same slice of our attention, and the same minute of our day.

Therefore, it is critical we develop and practice habits that assist us to be assertively direct and empathetic, while authentically managing our interactions. Too often conflicts and wasted time could be avoided if, in the first instance, we immediately conveyed our clear position, and immediately and constructively expressed our opinion. For example, we must feel comfortable and able to convey a simple and respectful 'no.'

Scared of Saying No?

One of the biggest obstacles to responsiveness is a fear of the consequences of saying no. In general, we are far keener to make contact to convey a positive, than we are to make contact to convey a negative.

Personally, I will always have greater respect for an individual that tells me a flat 'no thank you,' rather than being forced to listen to the sound of crickets chirping in the void of silence created by a non-response. When challenged as to why a response hasn't been provided, too often it is driven by a desire not to offend.

But this mind-set makes no sense. It declares that wasting a person's time and forcing them to continue to pursue a response with escalating frustration, is less offensive than providing a rebuttal – a simple 'thanks, but no thanks' response. Now that *is* bullshit.

When challenged further, the reality often includes a fear of saying no, as well as an inability to say no effectively – and stick to it. Therefore, declines in responsiveness are also created by a perceived inability to hold our ground. A fear that we will be too easily convinced to change to a 'yes.' In this context, non-responsiveness is used as a protective mechanism.

No matter the driver, the skill gap, or the underlying cause, not responding is poor form. In this world of multiple, complex, and nonstop demands, we need to be skilled at finishing our dialogues, and bringing our interactions to logical and clear conclusions.

We need to be comfortable saying 'no' to better manage our own time, as well as to convey respect for other's time. This shift will help underpin the development of a highly authentic and trusted personal brand.

Do We Care?

Unfortunately, there is another driver of non-responsiveness. It is selfishness. It is not caring about people's time. It's about a self-centred focus on personal needs. This is where an excessive focus on more, setting ridiculous and unrealistic goals, and creating self-centred materialistic aspirations, can all combine to drive selfish decision-making.

If the first question a person asks themselves about how (or if) to respond is: 'What's in it for me?' then consideration of the time and needs of others will be low on the importance list. Levels of responsiveness will plummet.

Technology Enablement

Another driver of poor responsiveness is technology enablement. Technology assists us to spew forth our demands and needs from anywhere, at any time. It de-personalises the request; it makes the recipient of our demands faceless. This in turn makes it far easier to ignore, and brush aside interactions with a person whom we have perhaps never met, never spoken to, and perhaps never will.

I have noticed over the years an increase in how sending a question from the safety of our keyboard reduces the level of personal responsibility to complete an interaction. There is an increase in the frequency of the "asker" feeling empowered and comfortable to ignore received responses.

Imagine initiating a face-to-face conversation, and then spontaneously standing up and walking off as the other party is mid-sentence in their answer. Without doubt, we would view this as rude. Yet, I see the equivalent of this occur in email and text interactions on a regular basis.

No matter the communication mode, no matter the communication platform used, we must operate with respect by considering the impact of what we are saying and not saying. To build a brand of responsiveness, we need to make sure that we acknowledge and respond to the information provided by others. Before throwing out a question or need, consider whether we will give the other party more of our time to complete the interaction.

The term 'keyboard warrior' invokes a sense of nameless individuals sending forth excessively negative criticism and personal attacks. But if we are not careful, it can be anyone. For it is also when we send out communications, and then fail to care enough to see them constructively and respectfully through to completion.

Chapter 19

The Alternative - Developing a Responsive Mindset

Completing Your Interactions

If we are too busy to acknowledge a response to our requests, or feel a topic simply doesn't warrant further input, then don't waste the other party's time in the first place by asking our questions or making our demands.

An attitude of 'they will know I got their answer,' must be removed. A mindset of 'they can work out I'm not interested,' must not be considered a reasonable end point.

> *If there is no intention to acknowledge the response, then don't ask the question.*

Silence doesn't represent an effective, clear, or respectful completion of an interaction. It is an irritant to others. And it's one of the countless little moments and actions that can negatively chip away at our professional brand.

Learn to Say No

Not responding only provides opportunity for the other party to make negative and uncomplimentary assumptions. On the other hand, a well delivered 'no' can strengthen relationships. It can achieve deeper understanding. And you know what else? It can stop a huge amount of time wasting.

There are several simple components to remember when saying no:

1. Be clear
2. Be direct (about what's relevant, in a constructive way, that does no harm)
3. Demonstrate empathy
4. Set clear expectations
5. If pushed, simply repeat what has already been said in a calm manner.

1. Be clear

Being clear on why we have made a 'no' decision is extremely important.

Too often a 'no' can be pushed, challenged, and subsequently worn down to a 'yes.' Not because of a lack of fortitude, or ability to stick with the original decision, but rather because it was a 'no' that was reached with a lack of comprehensive due diligence of all the related factors and variables. The position adopted then lacks a firm grounding from which the 'no' can be maintained. Without this grounding, the language used to convey our 'no' can lack clarity, and instead include ambiguity.

We must also appreciate that it is a strength to switch from a 'no' to a 'yes' when presented with new and critical information that changes the basis of our initial position. It is not a weakness. It suggests a holistic view, not a myopic decision-making perspective that refuses to shift with changes in the landscape.

2. Be direct

When making a 'no' statement it is critical we are direct in our communications. But remember, our directness must remain focused on what's relevant, in a constructive manner, that does no harm.

We should remove softening and distracting statements. We should focus on the key reason for why we are saying no. This need further reinforces the importance of the first component – being clear. The difference between the two statements 'I don't think I can probably do that' and 'I can't do that' are massive. Say each out loud. Feel the difference between the two.

The first is uncertain. The second is certain. The first gives pause for thought to challenge. The second is stronger and without ambiguity. The second conveys a definitive statement.

3. Demonstrate empathy

The use of empathy is critical to a successful outcome.

Empathetic statements demonstrate we have listened to a request. They also make it clear our 'no' response is based on having heard precisely what has been said. It is clear our response is not a preconceived thought. It is clear we have listened, processed the information, and then – and only then – have arrived at our conclusion.

Empathy also supports the level of active listening needed to determine if alternative actions or outcomes can be provided. It helps us stay focused and engaged should new information arise that would shift our position. Empathy also ensures we remain clear in our understanding of what we are saying 'no' to.

4. Set clear expectations

Setting unrealistic expectations for the future is an error that can be made in our attempts to soften a 'no' response.

This approach can be driven by feelings of guilt. False expectation-setting can in turn create uncertainty in our response that invites the other party to push and challenge our position. The classic 'I'm sorry I can't today, but any other day I'd be happy to' can back us into an unwanted corner. Is 'any other day' really an option to offer? These broad offerings can suggest an opening to take advantage of – an opportunity to exploit feelings of guilt to shift a 'no' to 'yes.'

Only offer viable alternatives if it is possible to do so. And only offer alternatives that can realistically be provided. Don't provide an impossible option, and then spend the following days or weeks attempting to avoid being held to account. That would be bullshit too!

5. Repeat

If we are excessively pushed to change our position, and remain certain it is the correct option, then it is important to feel empowered to hold our ground. This is achieved by re-stating our position clearly and firmly.

The key is to hold true to the core component of our message and repeat it calmly with both empathy and confidence. To repeat our key reason for saying no, balanced with ongoing empathy to demonstrate we are still listening.

Repeating the core reason for a 'no' also prevents us from throwing in other thoughts and ideas as they come to mind. The more information we attempt to add to support our position, the more it can sound like we are fumbling for excuses.

Further, the more we add, the longer the push back and arguing against our position will likely be.

Respectfully Saying 'No'

Reflect on each of the five components needed to convey an effective 'no.' How skilled are you at each? Which do you feel you do well? Which need to be strengthened?

Is it reducing the use of modifying softeners – words such as 'maybe,' 'perhaps,' and 'possibly'?

Is it only offering viable and constructive alternatives to avoiding being backed into a corner?

Know When to Walk Away

If our communications aren't working, and push back or arguing continues, we must also feel comfortable to walk away. To re-affirm our stated position, and then respectfully remove ourselves from the interaction.

Removing ourselves respectfully is achieved by not throwing departing hand grenades, such as 'I'll talk to you when you have calmed down.' These types of parting statements serve only to cause further irritation and argumentative responses.

Finally, of course, feel free to hit the "ignore button" if the other party will not relent in pushing their position. But be mindful of the next point.

Who We Ignore Today Could be Who We Need Tomorrow

No matter how big we think our pond, in today's world of connectivity and change there will always be a significant risk that the person we choose to ignore today, will be a person we critically need tomorrow. Again, approach all interactions with respect. If we are willing to use the precious time of others to request information, then afford them the respect of our time to respond.

Maybe it will be tomorrow, maybe next month, maybe next year, but that person we ignored today, will eventually repay the favour and ignore us when we need them most. When it comes to responsiveness, we reap tomorrow what we plant today. If we have planted a crop of rudeness, disconnect and silence, then be careful what tomorrow's crop will deliver.

The Impact on Your Personal Brand

We must remove dysfunctional strategies of ignoring and non-responsiveness from our repertoire. These must be replaced with timely responses and clear statements of intent and action – be it 'yes,' 'no,' or a respectfully delivered 'I will come back to you tomorrow.'

View every occasion where someone is ignored as the burning of a bridge. It may not always be a significant bridge, but it is a bridge all the same.

We must put the matches away, and make every interaction speak volumes of our professionalism. Make it a habit. Consider the brand you wish to convey, and then align all your behaviours and communications to support this brand.

Responsive? Respectful? Decisive? The choice is y*ours*.

Making these changes will help build a personal brand of responsiveness that embodies attributes of professionalism, trust, and integrity. It will also promote a no bullshit approach!

Developing a Responsive Personal Brand

What changes do you need to make to create a responsive personal brand?

What skills must be developed that will allow you to comfortably say no, and express your opinion in an assertive manner?

Do others perceive you as responsive and respectful of their time and effort?

Does your external self-awareness need to be strengthened to better understand the impact on others of your current level of responsiveness?

Chapter 20

The Misinterpretation of Body Language

An Abundance of Bullshit

Finally, a book focused on calling out bullshit must include a chapter on body language.

Why? Because it is without doubt, a topic that is overflowing with cliché advice, and widely known bullshit body language tips and tricks, that only result in misinterpretations and misunderstandings.

It is an area overflowing with self-proclaimed "experts" who are all too willing to share their masterful tips. Tips that lead to knowing how to *incorrectly* tell what a person is supposedly really thinking – irrespective of what they are saying!

Is Body Language Worth Considering?

In a word, yes. Has the interpretation of body language become warped and skewed? Also, yes.

We've typically heard a lot about body language. How our movements, posture and small, almost imperceptible, "tells" give away our *true* intent. How they give away our real opinion lurking just below the surface – an opinion that can appear through our subconscious actions.

But what if much of these interpretations were utter bullshit? What if many of the popular body language concepts have ignored critical points? Critical points, that if not carefully considered, make the attempted interpretation of body language a misguided and futile exercise.

The Potential for Misinterpretation

There are multiple examples of how the misinterpretation of body language can lead to poor outcomes and conflicts:

- Nodding of the head taken as agreement or understanding when none exists
- Clasping hands behind the head as a show of arrogance when none is felt
- Leaning back from a conversation as an attempt to withdraw when engagement remains.

But let's look in closer detail at one of the most widely misused markers for interpreting body language: the supposedly all-insightful folding of the arms.

The consensus is that the action of folding one's arms should be interpreted as an act of defensiveness – putting up a guard. A clear signal that the perpetrator is now withdrawn, angry, uncooperative, or guilty of a host of other negative assumptions.

But surely these negative assumptions must be fraught with error if there is insufficient context regarding an individual's past behaviours?

For any interpretation of body language to be robust and insightful, a baseline awareness is needed of how an individual typically interacts, responds, and moves.

When the negative assumptions of folded arms are challenged, there is also generally an acknowledgement that it is not the only plausible interpretation available. But there appears to be an ingrained, almost subconscious knee-jerk interpretation, to view those folded arms as an act of *defensiveness*, or further still, *defiance*.

Most definitely, for some people, in some situations, crossed arms *is* a mark of defensiveness. The notion here being that it is an instinctive action to place our arms as a barrier when made to feel threatened or uncomfortable. To be ready to protect our vital organs from possible attack.

But what then are other feasible interpretations?

- **Nothing.** The first and most likely interpretation to consider is nothing. Absolutely and utterly nothing to see here. Move along. Don't stress. For many people (myself included) crossing their arms is an act of comfort. It is nothing to do with a subconscious desire to flee, or an attempt to stop our 'fight-or-flight' mechanism kicking in. It is purely and simply a more comfortable option than having our arms flail loosely at our sides. It is a far better option than letting our arms hang awkwardly as we attempt to resist crossing them to avoid a misinterpretation of defensiveness.
- **Cold.** Another highly plausible interpretation is that the individual is cold. Crossing our arms tightly is

a great way to help keep warm. I've lost count of the number of times I have walked into a workshop, only to be greeted by a set of less than happy faces sitting with arms tightly crossed. Are they unhappy at the prospects of having to sit through a day-long session with me? No (well I hope not). Instead, the maintenance team hadn't fixed the thermostat in the room. The result? The air conditioner spewing forth a howling Siberian wind!

- **Concentrating.** Those crossed arms can also be a mark of concentration. This is one habit that I know I personally have. I also frequently combine it with sitting back and looking up towards the ceiling. It has nothing to do with defensiveness or disengaging. It is all about a thinking posture as I reflect deeply on a specific point.
- **Who Knows?** Finally, there are some for whom the action of crossing their arms is simply an idiosyncrasy unique to the individual. It could be a way of dealing with a bad odour, a sign of tiredness, or a reaction to a recent argument that is still being replayed in their mind. But certainly, it is not related to defensiveness.

Consider all the other body language signals we have been taught to look for, and then interpret in specific ways. How many alternative options exist for each that has nothing whatsoever to do with the popularised interpretation?

If it's comfortable to cross your arms, do so. If it is comfortable to sit or stand with those arms comfortably folded and resting on your stomach, then do it.

But we must also be wary that our actions, such as arm folding, will be prone to misinterpretation. Therefore, at times we must make considered choices about when to modify our body language to remove the potential for mixed messages caused by poor interpretations. More on that one shortly.

Poor Alignment of Body Language, Words and Tone

Consideration of our body language, tone, and choice of words should be central to the development of our communication skills. We should be aware of how these three components of our communications help to create the whole message.

I have observed many situations where a poor alignment between these three components has resulted in the delivery of very disconnected messages: messages lacking impact, and messages lacking authenticity. One of the most memorable examples I have observed of this poor alignment was demonstrated by the CEO of an organisation.

A presentation was delivered that was intended to motivate, uplift and inspire staff. It was to convey a sense of excitement about the company's future. To provide an overview of what was in the pipeline, where the company was headed, and give a sense of how staff were to be engaged and connected with the corporate vision.

The CEO's message was compelling and inspiring. The presentation was well rehearsed, yet comfortable. The technology was well-balanced and conveyed a sense of professionalism without distracting from the message. The CEO was well-spoken, maintained strong eye contact, and demonstrated all the skills of a confident, and well-practiced, presenter and speaker.

But it was the body language at the very end of the presentation that undermined much of the message that preceded it. The final statements were delivered with flourish and inspiration. But, instead of remaining present to answer questions and truly connect with staff, the CEO abruptly left. As the last words reached the audience, the CEO promptly turned, walked briskly to the side of the room, picked up a glass of water, drank it in one long take, and then walked straight out through a side exit.

Most staff didn't appear to notice. Luckily, they were focused elsewhere on back slaps and high fives about how great their organisation was. But for me, it left an overpowering sense that the CEO had somewhere better to be. That the "communicate with staff" box had just been ticked. 'Check – now they will be happy for another year. And now, I'm off to something far more interesting than my staff.'

It was a missed opportunity to reinforce the words spoken by staying physically present for a few extra minutes. It was a set of actions that were a complete contradiction to everything said before.

It is therefore critical to ensure our actions, words and tone of delivery are all well-aligned – from the very first word and action to the last. Irrespective of how stressed or busy we may be, to achieve the greatest and most positive impact, our body language, tone and words must be congruent and collectively heading in the same direction.

It is this alignment that is a key ingredient needed to convey the critical elements of genuineness, authenticity and respect. But it is an alignment that can too frequently be lacking.

The Power Stance

Another piece of body language bullshit, and one that has gained significant traction in recent years, is the concept of a "power stance." The stance to adopt when we aim to exude confidence and authority. The stance to adopt when in front of an audience or networking. A stance to leave a positive and memorable impression.

What is it? It is a stance that requires our feet be approximately shoulder width apart. Our weight centred slightly forward on the balls of our feet. Our back upright and standing tall. Our hands placed on our hips. Our head held up straight with strong and direct eye contact at our prey. Sorry, I mean audience!

Try it out. Stand in front of a mirror and see how it looks. Does it make you feel confident? Does it make you look as though you really know what you are talking about?

On the contrary, it can create an arrogant and superior looking disposition. It is heavily biased towards masculine and extroverted stereotypes. But guess what? Clearly, we aren't all masculine, and we aren't all extroverts. Certainly, not everyone wants to be an extrovert. And most definitely, not everyone feels a need to radiate masculinity!

Yet this stance is presented by "experts" as a means to convey confidence and authority. To positively shift a less confident mindset and increase levels of self-belief. But if it feels uncomfortable, and unnatural, it can have a disastrous and opposite effect. It can feel like putting on an exceptionally ill-fitted suit. It can, in fact, make us feel more self-conscious and awkward.

Absolutely, we should avoid a nervous driven posture that conveys fear or anxiety: staring at our feet, wringing our hands, and fidgeting. But surely, we can find a better option. A posture that makes us feel comfortable and relaxed, while appearing engaging and authentic.

Chapter 21

The Alternative - Context and Patterns

The Collaborative Stance

The power stance is exactly what the name suggests.

If we are wanting to stand so that our posture and presence is about having power over others, then go for it. But if we are seeking a stance that engages and connects, then consider what I call the *Collaborative Stance*.

By contrast, this is a stance that is comfortable. A stance that engages and connects with our audience. A stance that gives out signals of 'I'm present, I'm engaged, and I'm listening.' It should involve good eye contact, some degree of movement that supports our active listening, and it must suit the situation.

What should this look like exactly? That is up to the individual. It most definitely shouldn't be a 'one size fits all' concept. We must each find our own personal sweet spot.

Find what works well for you. Find what "fits" comfortably, is genuine, and engages and connects with your audience. You will most definitely know it when you find it.

Acutely Tune-in

There are times when coaching participants have thought I held mind reading skills. An ability to pick up true feelings and perspectives on a topic or situation before much detail had been provided.

Nothing could be further from the truth. Instead, it is about acutely tuning-in to the interaction. When communicating, I focus on what the person is saying. What questions they answer. How they answer. Which questions they avoid, or quickly skip over. All the while, monitoring their body language as they talk. If we pay highly focused attention, and listen with an open mind, instead of adopting ill-conceived notions of body language, there is a rich abundance of information to be had.

Understanding Your Transparency

All too often, we are far more transparent in our thinking and opinions than we realise. At times, the conflicting signals are blatantly obvious: contradictions between what we outwardly claim, and an opposing opinion we hold internally. In these moments, it can be all too easy to detect what is furiously bubbling away just below the surface. But without a mirror before us, how can we effectively self-monitor, and know when our body language is giving away opinions we think are being successfully suppressed?

We must always imagine that our surface behaviours are resting on the magma of our deeper opinions and feelings. The only way to prevent minor or major volcanic eruptions of that magma is to develop strategies that support constructively expressing our opinions, our concerns, and our needs.

We must develop constructive strategies that allow us to *choose* to let something go, as opposed to feeling something must be let go because of an inability to act. Correctly determining what is within our control, and what is outside our control, will assist in the development of genuine communications that are supported by well-aligned opinions, behaviours, and therefore body language. It will also assist prevent emotional eruptions.

Refer back to Chapter 7 for ideas on how to become more self-aware to support this.

Context

Context is one of the most crucial perspectives overlooked when interpreting body language.

Context highlights the need to consider the where, when, and how of a specific gesture, pose or movement. Take my example of arriving to find workshop participants sitting with arms crossed: the key context point is the air conditioner pumping out a cold Siberian wind.

Consider a candidate sitting awkwardly on the edge of their chair in a job interview. Are they nervous? Alternatively, the missed context may be a lower back complaint, lived with for so many years, they no longer realise their posture unintentionally conveys nervousness.

Without context, the successful interpretation of body language is seriously compromised and fraught with danger.

Know the context before interpreting body language.

The notion that we are able to learn skills that will allow us to walk into a crowded room and quickly, skillfully, and accurately read the mood must also be considered bullshit. Without context, all we are performing is an act of gross generalisation to fit incomplete information into a flawed interpretation framework. Flawed because it is also incomplete. Flawed because it is based on concepts that may, or may not, hold true. Without context, who knows? And yet, I have heard many, many stories of people trained in how to do just this.

Patterns

Our pattern of behaviour is the next important perspective that is too often overlooked when interpreting body language.

Our patterns of body language refer to an individual's own set of unique and personal body language habits. It provides a baseline of behaviour from which to interpret. This level of specific knowledge, and personal insight, enables the observer to identify behaviours that are a departure from the norm – those behaviours that will support insightful interpretation. It also allows the observer to establish robust connections between body language behaviours and specific mindsets.

Know the patterns before interpreting body language.

I have read many examples of body language interpretation committed with neither context nor pattern by self-proclaimed "body language experts." But one example stands out most in my memory for its level of absurdity.

The body language of a very high-profile, internationally renowned CEO was interpreted from the footage taken of a formal presentation. The "body language expert" would have had no personal dealings with the CEO. There would have been limited opportunities, if any, to observe prior actions and behaviours beyond highly scripted public presentations and speeches: highly scripted company announcements, not free-flowing and unscripted behaviours that would have occurred in an unguarded or relaxed moment.

In short, next to no valid observations could be made of natural behaviours in order to understand the CEO's personal context or patterns.

From the footage, the "body language expert" had determined the CEO's performance to be highly thought through and choreographed – that bit was obvious. CEO media presentations always are!

But it was further noted that the speech was delivered seated. It was also noted the CEO was leaning slightly forward, hands firmly planted as anchors on the desk he was seated at to reduce unwanted movement. A posture and demeanour that was determined to have been carefully orchestrated to convey a high degree of seriousness. It was even noted a pillow had been used on the seat to give the CEO greater height, and thus convey an even greater sense of authority and knowledge. All these points were interpreted as purposeful actions taken to assert influence and superiority into the dialogue. Actions to exude strength and power.

All this may have been true. But with absolutely no context, and without any clear pattern to judge from, an equally plausible and accurate interpretation would be that the CEO was recovering from a fresh case of extremely uncomfortable haemorrhoids.

Likely? I don't know. Bullshit. Perhaps. But that is precisely my point: without further information, the body language expert could be no more confident in their interpretation than I could be in mine.

From the observed information alone, a case of haemorrhoids is just as plausible as what was proposed.

The Bigger Picture

It is also critical to understand the broader perspective, or bigger picture, before interpreting body language. This is a combination of both the *context* and the *pattern*. It can assist us determine if what we are perceiving is insightful and valuable, or whether it is short lived. Is it only a minor behavioural hiccup that tells little, and means even less?

This bigger picture perspective should also challenge us to consider broader factors. For example, one broader factor worth considering is cultural context.

A firm handshake in one culture may be a sign of strength. While in another, a blatant attempt to intimidate. Standing so close to someone that we can distinctly smell last night's garlic laced dish may be fine in one culture, but way too close for comfort in another.

Taking Control of Your Message

Finally, it is important that we not only work to remove bullshit interpretations of the behaviours and actions of *others*, but also never forget that bullshit interpretations are frequently being assigned to *our* actions and behaviours.

We must be aware of all the pitfalls of misinterpretation being applied to us. Although our folded arms may be comfortable and relaxing, it's important to consider when and where this may be misconstrued to mean something different. It is crucial to consider when and where this misinterpretation will harm our interactions, or place obstacles before us that we must subsequently overcome.

Therefore, the most effective way to take control of our own body language is to avoid being caught out by the cliché and poor misinterpretation pitfalls committed by others.

To convey a positive and engaging approach we should consider:

- Maintaining good eye contact
- Using engaging and reaffirming movements, such as head nods, that demonstrate we are focused
- Keeping our hands free of distractions, such as clicking pens, so that they can be used to reinforce our opinions with constructive and supportive gestures
- Leaning slightly forward and sitting upright in our chair
- Avoiding crossed arms in key moments – particularly if there is a high chance of an interpretation of defensiveness.

Improving Your Body Language

Take time to reflect on your own body language habits. Consider both your own habits, as well as the opinions and generalisations you have used when interpreting the behaviours of others.

What needs to change? Can you maintain a 'poker face,' when required? Alternatively, are you an open book laid bare for all to read? Or should that be misread?

Chapter 22

In Conclusion - The Way Forward

Switch on Your Bullshit-O-Meter

If it smells like it, looks like it, and there is a bull standing right next to it – then it is highly likely to be bullshit.

But can you effectively identify bullshit without multiple and obvious indicators? And once you have identified something as bullshit, do you have a constructive alternative to turn to?

Now that you have read this book, I challenge you to critically assess the information and advice that abounds around you. To then create and embed beneficial, sensible, and authentic alternatives.

Consider what actions and communications will enrich and improve your life. Consider what will enrich the lives of others, or, at the very least, do no harm.

Can you recognise whether your mindset and goals are based excessively on self-serving and materialistic practices? Are you on a path that will lead to self-damage created by the pursuit of unrealistic expectations, and unsustainable – or even unachievable – goals and objectives? Worse still, are they goals and objectives that can only be achieved by walking over others?

Be More Critical

To assist in this self-reflection, we need to be significantly more critical and analytical in our appraisal of what we see and hear. It is crucial we no longer passively swallow information presented to us.

How does a piece of new information sit with what we already know? Does it connect with, and extend, our current knowledge bank of information, or does it grate against it? Is this grating because we have identified held knowledge and ideas that need updating? Is it because the new information needs to be rejected, or further investigated?

> *We need to take healthier sized bites and chew longer, so that we can effectively digest information to determine its veracity and its palatability.*

We are outsourcing our ability to effectively critique information to internet search engines, and by extension, there has become an increased level of naivety to swallow without chewing – to not challenge, investigate and discern sufficiently. Internet search engines are amazing tools. But the information presented in response to our searches is neither filtered nor evaluated by any measure of bullshit. That bit is up to you.

It is up to you to discern fact from fiction. To distinguish flawed advice or information, from constructive advice or information.

Which brings me to one of my favourite quotes on the internet:

> *'The problem with internet quotes is that you can't always depend on their accuracy.'*

Abraham Lincoln, 1864

Give More Feedback

Personally, I love the notion of criticizing something.

It creates deeper thought and analysis of information. But it is intriguing how the action of criticizing has developed a negative connotation. An interesting and simple exercise is to tell someone 'I'm going to criticize you.' Watch the person's immediate reactions. Watch their facial expressions and their body language. Typically, there is now a degree of defensiveness, a readiness to hit back with a rebuttal.

But next, tell them 'I thought what you just did was absolutely brilliant, and I greatly appreciate the effort you demonstrated.' Now note their reaction. It's typically a mix of confusion and surprise.

To criticize is to give feedback. Yet the act of giving criticism has morphed into an assumed negative and harbinger of bad news. It is not. To criticize is to *evaluate*. It is to assess the merit, quality, and value of something, so that we can then provide an insightful opinion. It is a key component of learning. It is a pivotal component needed for spotting and removing bullshit.

As part of your way forward, you must reclaim the positive notion of criticism. You must aim to be as comfortable providing it, as you are comfortable receiving it. You must be more critical, and feel at ease, to push back against the information you are bombarded with day in and day out.

Acquiring a critical mindset is a core ingredient needed to stem the flow of poor and misleading bullshit in our lives.

Call out Bullshit from this Day Forth

When you see and hear bullshit, don't let it slide. Look to challenge its logic, both assertively and constructively.

Ask key questions to challenge yourself and its source:

- Does it make sense?
- Does it really create sustainable and long-term benefits – for me, for others?
- Will it genuinely help make me happier, wiser, and productive?

The ball is now in your court.

This book has provided you with motives and opportunities to self-reflect and self-challenge to reevaluate various aspects of life. To reflect on where you have come from. And to critically look forward to where your actions, behaviours and mindset are currently taking you.

It is now up to you to seize the moment.

Are you truly on a constructive and healthy life path, or are you aiming for an idealised destination?

Is it a destination you can reach? Is it even a destination you really wish to reach?

As John Monash, an Australian civilian engineer and military commander, surmised it:

> 'Adopt as your fundamental creed that you will equip yourself for life, not solely for your own benefit, but for the benefit of the whole community.'
>
> John Monash

Now join me – call out and reject *Bullshit*!

www.ingramcontent.com/pod-product-compliance
Lightning Source LLC
Chambersburg PA
CBHW071353290426
44108CB00014B/1534